1694-1778 Voltaire

The history of the Russian empire under Peter the Great

1694-1778 Voltaire

The history of the Russian empire under Peter the Great

ISBN/EAN: 9783741182815

Manufactured in Europe, USA, Canada, Australia, Japa

Cover: Foto ©ninafisch / pixelio.de

Manufactured and distributed by brebook publishing software (www.brebook.com)

1694-1778 Voltaire

The history of the Russian empire under Peter the Great

THE
HISTORY
OF THE
RUSSIAN EMPIRE
UNDER
Peter the Great.

Newly translated from the French

OF

M. DE VOLTAIRE.

IN TWO VOLUMES.

VOLUME II.

PUBLISHED FROM A MANUSCRIPT SENT HIM BY THE COURT OF PETERSBURG.

LONDON:
Sold by A. MILLAR, J. HODGES, D. MIDWINTER, M. COOPER, and J. and R. TONSON.

MDCCLXXVIII.

THE CONTENTS.

To the reader,   page i

PART. II. CHAP. I.

Campaign of Pruth,   1

CHAP. II.

Conclusion of the affair of Pruth.   31

CHAP. III.

Marriage of the Czarowitz; and solemn declaration of Peter's marriage with Catherine. Her brother makes himself known.   37

CHAP. IV.

Stetin taken. Descent upon Finland. Events of the year 1714.   47

VOL. II.   CHAP.

CHAP. V.

Successes of Peter the Great. Charles XII. returns into his dominions, 67

CHAP. VI.

State of Europe at the return of Charles XII. Siege of Stralsund, 75

CHAP. VII.

Wismar taken. New travels of the Czar, 81

CHAP. VIII.

Continuation of the travels of Peter the Great, Goertz's conspiracy. Reception of Peter in France, 87

CHAP. IX.

Of the return of the Czar to his dominions. Of his policy and occupations, 99

CHAP. X.

Trial and condemnation of prince Alexis Petrowitz, 105

CONTENTS

CHAP. XI.

Works and establishments in 1717, and the following years, 145

CHAP. XII.

Of the trade of Russia.
Of the trade with China.
Of the trade of Petersburg, and the other parts of the Russian empire, 151

CHAP. XIII.

Of the laws. 158

CHAP. XIV.

Of religion. 161

CHAP. XV.

Negotiations in the isle of Aland. Death of Charles XII. The treaty of Nystadt. 170

CHAP. XVI.

Conquests in Persia. 180

CHAP.

CONTENTS.

CHAP. XVII.

Of the Coronation of the Empress Catherine I and the Death of Peter the Great. 195

ORIGINAL PIECES.

Condemnation of Alexis, June twenty-fourth 1718, 206
The peace of Nystadt, 212
Proclamation of the Emperor Peter I. for the coronation of the Empress Catherine, 230

TO THE
READER.

IN our time the empire of Ruſſia is become of ſuch conſequence in Europe, that the hiſtory of its founder, Peter the Great, becomes the more intereſting, as it is he who has given a new face to the north; and ſince his death, his empire has been upon the point of giving a new turn to the fate of Germany; his influence having extended itſelf over France and Spain, notwithſtanding the great diſtance of theſe places.

THE eſtabliſhment of this empire is perhaps the epocha of the moſt importance to Europe; and it is this ſolely which engages the author of the fiſt part of the hiſtory of Peter the Great, to publiſh the ſecond.

THERE are ſome errors in the firſt part, of which it is neceſſary to give the reader notice, and are as follows: page 23, after the words *in the route which the caravans might take through independent Tartary,* add *in travelling through the Calmuck plains, and over the great deſert of Kobi* Page 37, for *Red Ruſſia,* read *with a part of Red Ruſſia.*

And here it may not be improper to acquaint those critics, who know little of the matter, that Volhinia, Podolia, and some of the neighbouring countries, have been named Red Russia by all geographers. Page 65, after the words, *when the Greek church was established in Russia*, take out what follows, and in its place insert, *Chrysoberg, patriarch of Constantinople, sent a bishop to baptize Wolodimer, in order that he might, by that means, add this part of the world to his patriarchal see. Wolodimer then finished the work that had been begun by his father. One Michael, a native of Syria, was the first Metropolitan of Russia* Page 70, *He considered the Jesuits as dangerous politicians;* to which may be added, that the Jesuits, who introduced themselves into Russia in the year 1685, were expelled from that empire again in 1689, and having a second time got footing, they were again driven out in 1718.

The appellation of *small* may be left to the country of Orenburg, because that government is small in comparison of Siberia, on which it borders. For *the skin of a sheep*, which some travellers affirm to be worshipped by the Ostiacks, may be substituted that of a *bear*: for if these good people pay divine worship to a thing, because it is useful to them, the fur of a bear is still more adorable; but he must wear an ass's skin who lays so much weight upon such trifles.

Whether the barks constructed by Peter I. were or were not called *half galleys*, or whether this prince dwelt at first in a wooden, or a brick house,

house, will, I believe, be thought of little signification.

THERE are some things less unworthy of the attention of a judicious reader. It is said, for example, in the first volume, that the people of Kamtshatka are without religion; but some recent memoirs inform me, that these savage people have their divines as well as we, who make the inhabitants of this peninsula to be descended from a superior being, whom they call *Kouthou*. These memorials say, that they pay no worship to him, and that they neither love nor fear him.

HENCE it appears, that though they have a mythology, yet they have no religion; this may be true, but it is not very probable. Fear is the natural attribute of man. It is said, in the midst of their absurdities, they distinguish things allowed, and things forbidden; among the former they reckon the indulging of the passions; and, among the latter, the sharpening a knife or a hatchet while they are travelling, or the saving a person from drowning: but if it is held a sin by these people, to save the life of a fellow creature when in danger, they are in that respect certainly different from all other people in the universe, who instinctively run to the assistance of each other, when interest and passion suppresses not their natural inclination. One would imagine, that they could never have thought of making an action criminal, which in itself is so common and necessary, that it is even meritorious, but by a philosophy equally false and superstitious, which would inculcate, that we are not in any thing to oppose destiny, and that no one ought to save a man from being drowned whom God has pre-ordained to be so: but these barbarians have not the least knowledge even of a false philosophy; and yet we are told, that they celebrate a great feast, which they call by a word, which in their language signifies *purification:* but from what are they to purify themselves, if they hold every thing to be permitted to them? and for what, if they neither fear nor love their god *Kouthou?*

THEIR notions are, doubtless, in many particulars contradictory, as are indeed those of almost every other people; with this difference, that theirs arise from a want of understanding, ours from an abuse of it. We abound much more in contradictions, because we reason much more.

As they acknowledge a kind of God, so they have also their devils. Lastly, they have also sorcerers and magicians amongst them, as there have always been amongst all nations, even the most polished. In Kamtschatka, old women are looked upon to be witches, as they were amongst us, till we had attained a clear knowledge of natural philosophy. Hence, we find, it has ever been the lot of human understanding, to entertain absurd notions, founded on our curiosity and on our weakness. The people of Kamptschatka have also their prophets, who interpret their dreams; and it is not long since we had such amongst us.

AFTER the court of Russia had subdued these people, by erecting five fortresses in their country, they instituted the Christian religion of the Greek church

church amongst them. A Russian gentleman, perfectly well acquainted with these people, informed me, that one of their greatest objections to receiving it was, that they were certain it could not be instituted for them, in as much as bread and wine were essential parts of our holy rites, whereas they had neither bread nor wine in their country.

These people, in other respects, deserve very little notice. I shall observe one thing with respect to them, namely, that if we survey the three fourths of America, the whole southern part of Africa, and the north from Lapland as far as the sea of Japan, we shall find one half of mankind to be very little superior to the people of Kamtschatka.

And here it may not be amiss to observe to the reader, that the celebrated geographer De L'Isle calls this country Kamtshat, as the French and Italians commonly retrench the *ka* and *kay*, which terminate most of the Russian names.

But there is a more important article which may concern the dignity of crowned heads. Olearius, who, in 1634, accompanied the envoys of Holstein into Russia and Persia, relates in the third book of his history, that Czar Iwan Basilowitz banished the emperor's ambassador into Siberia. This is a fact which I do not remember to have found mentioned by any other historian. It is hardly probable that the emperor would have quietly submitted to so extraordinary an insult, and open violation of the law of nations.

The same Olearius says, in another place, "We set out on the thirteenth of February 1634, in company with an ambaffador from the court of France, called the count of Tallerand, and prince of Chalais, &c. who had been fent by Lewis, together with one James Rouffel, on an embaffy to Turky and Mufcovy; but his collegue did him fo many ill turns with the patriarch of Ruffia, that the great duke banifhed him into Siberia."

In the third book he fays, that this ambaffador, the prince of Chalais, and Rouffel his collegue, who was a merchant, were fent as envoys by Henry IV. It is not very probable that Henry IV. who died in 1610, fhould have fent an embaffy to Ruffia in 1634; and if Lewis XIII. had fent as an ambaffador, a perfon of fo illuftrious a houfe as that of Tallerand, he would hardly have given him a merchant for his collegue; all Europe would have known of this embaffy, and an infult of fo fingular a nature offered to the king of France would have made ftill more noife.

Having difputed this improbable fact in the firft part of this hiftory; but finding that it continued to gain fome credit, I thought it neceffary to fearch the regifter of foreign affairs in France, for clearer information on this head; and find that the following incident gave rife to this miftake of Olearius.

There was indeed a perfon of the family of Tallerand, who, being very fond of travelling, made a voyage into Turky, without acquainting his family of his intention, or furnifhing himfelf with the neceffary letters of recommendation. At the court of Mofcow, he met with a Dutch merchant named Rouffel, who acted as agent for a company

of

of merchants, who had a correspondence with the French ministry. The marquis of Tallerand kept company with this man, in order to go on a tour to Persia; but having had some dispute with his fellow traveller by the way, this latter accused him falsely to the patriarch of Moscow; and he was actually banished into Siberia. However, having found means to make his situation known to his family, at the end of about three years, Mr. Des Noyers, secretary of state, obtained his discharge from the court of Moscow.

This is the real state of the fact, and which would not deserve a place in history, but as it may serve to put the reader upon his guard against the multitude of anecdotes of a like nature, which the relations of most travellers abound with.

There are historical errors, and historical falshoods. What Olearius relates is only an error; but when we are told, that a Czar made an ambassador's hat be nailed to his head, that is a falshood. A writer may be mistaken, in regard to the number or force of the ships that compose a naval armament, or with respect to the extent of a country; but these only are errors, and of a very excusable kind. Again, those who repeat the fabulous accounts of antiquity, in which the origin of all nations is enveloped, may be accused of a weakness common to all the writers of old times; but this is not falsifying, it is, properly speaking, no more than transcribing tales.

Inadvertency also leads us into several mistakes, which cannot be called lies: for example, when

when we read in Hubner's new geography, that the boundaries of Europe are in that place where the river Oby enters into the Black fea, and that Europe contains thirty millions of inhabitants; thefe are inaccuracies, which an intelligent reader can eafily rectify

The fame treatife frequently prefents us with large towns ftrongly fortified and very populous, which are in reality no other than infignificant villages, in a manner uninhabited. But here it is eafily feen that time has totally changed the face of things; that the author has confulted only ancient writers, and that what was matter of fact in their time, ceafes to be fo at prefent.

Some writers again are miftaken in the inferences they draw from facts. Peter the great fuppreffed the patriarchal dignity. Hubner adds, that he made himfelf be declared patriarch. Certain fpurious hiftories of Ruffia go further, and fay, that he officiated in the pontifical character. Thus, from a known fact, they have drawn erroneous conclufions, which happen but too often.

What I have called hiftorical falfhoods, is ftill more common, and is the invention of flattery, or a foolifh love for the marvellous. The hiftorian who, to ingratiate himfelf with a powerful family, proftitutes his pen to praife a tyrant, is a bafe wretch; he who endeavours to blaft the memory of a good prince, is a villain; and the romancer who publifhes the inventions of his own brain, for real facts, is a defpicable creature. The man who in former times made whole nations pay reverence to his fables, would now hardly be read by the populace.

There are some critics who deal still deeper in falshood: such are those who alter passages, or else misconstrue them; and who, promoted by envy, ignorantly carp at works of real utility: but let us leave those vipers to gnaw the file, let them even go on.

THE HISTORY OF THE RUSSIAN EMPIRE UNDER PETER THE GREAT

PART THE SECOND

CHAP. I.

Campaign of Pruth.

THE Sultan Achmet III. proclaimed war against Peter I. not from a regard of serving Charles, but merely from a view to serve his own interest. The Khan of Crim Tartary saw, with fear, a neighbour become so powerful as Peter I. The Porte had, for some time, taken umbrage at the number of the vessels

which

which this prince had on the Palus Mæotis, and upon the Black sea, at his fortifying the city of Asoph, and at the flourishing state of the harbour of Taganroc, already become famous; in short, at his great series of successes, and the ambition which success always increases.

It is neither probable nor true, that the Porte should have begun the war against the Czar, on the Palus Mæotis, because a Swedish ship had taken a bark on the Baltic sea, on board of which was found a letter of a minister, whose name has hitherto been kept secret. Norberg tells us, that this letter contained a plan for the conquest of the Turkish empire; that it was carried to Charles XII. who was then in Turky, and was by him sent to the divan; and that this was the cause why war was declared. But the absurdity of this is seen at first sight. It was the remonstrances of the Khan of Tartary, who was more uneasy about the neighbourhood of Asoph than the Turkish divan, that induced the latter to give orders for the Ottoman forces to take the field *.

* The account this chaplain gives of the demands of the Grand Signior is equally false and puerile He says that the Sultan Achmet, previous to his declaring war against the Czar, sent to that prince a paper containing the conditions on which he was willing to grant him peace. These conditions, Norberg informs us, were as follows: "That Peter should renounce his alliance with Augustus, reinstate Stanislaus in the possession of the crown of Poland, restore all Livonia to Charles XII and pay that prince the value in ready money of what he had taken from him at the battle o Pultowa; and lastly that the Czar should demolish his newly bul: city of Petersburg." This piece was forged by one Crazey, a half starved pamphleteer, and author of a

It

IT was the month of August, and before the Czar had compleatly reduced Livonia, when Achmet III. resolved to declare war against him. The Turks, at that time, could hardly have had the news of the taking of Riga, and, therefore, the proposal of restoring to the king of Sweden the value in money, of the effects he had lost at the battle of Pultowa, would have been as ridiculous a thing as that of demolishing Petersburg The behaviour of Charles XII. at Bender, was sufficiently romantic ; but the conduct of the Turkish divan would have been much more so, if we suppose it to have insisted upon any such things.

THE khan of Tartary, who was the principal instigator of this war, went and paid a visit to Charles at Bender *. They were connected by the same interests, inasmuch as Asoph makes part of the frontiers of Little Tartary. Charles and the khan were the two greatest sufferers by the victories of the Czar; but the khan did not command the forces of the Grand Signior. He was like one of the feudatory princes of Germany, who served in the armies of the empire, with their own troops, and were subject to the authority of the general in chief of the imperial army.

THE first step the divan took †, was to arrest Tolstoy, the Czar's ambassador, in the streets of Constantinople, together with thirty of his domesticks,

work intitled, Memoirs satyrical, historical, and entertaining. It was from his fountain Norberg drew his intelligence, and however he may have been the confessor of Charles XII. he certainly does not appear to have been his confident.
  * Nov. 1710.   † Nov. 29 1710.

who

who with their master were all committed to the prison of the Seven Towers. This barbarous custom which would make even savages blush, is owing to the Turks having always a number of foreign ministers residing amongst them from other courts, whereas they never send any in return. They look upon the ambassadors of the Christian princes in no other light than as merchants or consuls; and having naturally as great a contempt for Christians as they have for Jews, they seldom condescend to observe the laws of nations, in respect of them, unless forced to it; at least, they have hitherto persisted in this barbarous haughtiness.

The celebrated vizir Achmet Cuprogli, he who took the island of Candia, under Mahomet IV. behaved rudely to the son of the French ambassador, and even carried his brutality so far as to strike him, and afterwards to commit him to prison, without Lewis XIV. proud and lofty as he was, daring to resent it, otherwise than by sending another minister to the Porte. The Christian princes, who are extremely delicate on the point of honour amongst themselves, and have made it a part of the law of nations, seem to be totally indifferent to this, with regard to the Turks.

No sovereign ever suffered greater affronts in the persons of his ministers, than Czar Peter. In the space of a few years his ambassador at the court of London was thrown into jail for debt, his plenipotentiary at the courts of Poland and Saxony was broke upon the wheel, by order of the king of Sweden; and now his minister at the Ottoman Porte was

was seized and thrown into a dungeon at Constantinople, like a common malefactor.

It has been observed, in the first part of this history, that he received satisfaction from England, for the insult offered to his ambassador at London. The horrible affront he suffered in the person of Patkul, was washed away in the blood of the Swedes slain at the battle of Pultowa; but they could never chastise the Turks for the violation of the law of nations.

The Czar was forced to quit the theatre of the war in the west ‡, in order to fight on the frontiers of Turky. He began by causing ten regiments, which he had in Poland, to advance towards Moldavia *. He then gave orders for marshal Scheremetow to set out from Livonia, with his body of troops, and, leaving prince Menzikoff at the head of affairs at Petersburg, he returned to Moscow, to give orders for the ensuing campaign.

He next fixed a senate of regency ¶, ordered the regiment of guards to begin their march, and all the young nobility to follow him to the field, to learn the art of war, placing some of them in the station of cadets, and others in that of subaltern officers. Admiral Apraxin was sent to take the command by sea and land. All these several measures being concerted, Peter gives orders for acknowledging a new empress. This was the very person who had been taken prisoner in Marienburg, in the year

‡ Jan. 1711.
* It is very strange that so many writers always confound Walacia and Moldavia together. ¶ Jan. 18.

1702.

1702. Peter had, in 1696, repudiated his wife Eudoxia Lapoukin, by whom he had two children. The canons of his church allow of divorces; but had they not, Peter would have paſſed a law to permit them.

The fair captive of Marienburg, who had taken the name of Catherine, had a ſoul ſuperior to her ſex and her misfortunes. Her behaviour had made her ſo agreeable to the Czar, that he would have her always near his perſon. She accompanied him in all his travels, and moſt fatiguing campaigns; ſharing in his toils, and alleviating his cares by her natural cheerfulneſs, and the great attention ſhe ſhewed to oblige him on all occaſions, and the little regard ſhe expreſſed for the luxury, dreſs, and other indulgences, which the generality of her ſex in other countries make real neceſſities. But what rendered her a more extraordinary favourite, was her neither being envied nor oppoſed, nor was any other perſon ſacrificed to make room for her promotion. She frequently ſoftened the Czar's wrath, and by making him more merciful, added to his greatneſs. In fine, ſhe became ſo neceſſary to him, that he married her privately, in 1707. He had already two daughters by her, and the following year ſhe bore him a third, who was afterwards married to the duke of Holſtein *.

The Czar made his private marriage known the very day he ſet out with her to fight againſt the Turks †. The ſeveral diſpoſitions he had made

---

* March 17, 1711. † The journal of Peter the Great.

ſeemed

seemed to promise a succesful campaign. The hetman of the Cossacks was to keep the Tartars in awe, who had already begun to make incursions into the Ukraine. The main body of the Russian army was advancing towards Neister, and another body of troops, under prince Galitzin, were in full march through Poland. Every thing went on favourably at the beginning; for Galitzin having met with a numerous body of Tartars near Kiow, who had been joined by some Cossacks and some Poles of king Staniflaus's party, as also a few Swedes, he defeated them entirely, and killed near five thousand men. These Tartars had, in their march through the open country, made about ten thousand prisoners. It has been the custom of the Tartars, time immemorial, to carry with them a much greater number of cords than scimitars, in order to bind the unhappy prisoners they take. The captives were all set free, and those who had made them prisoners were put to the sword. The whole Russian army, if it had been assembled together, would have amounted to sixty thousand men. It was to have been farther augmented by the troops belonging to the king of Poland. This prince, who owed every thing to the Czar, came to pay him a visit at Jarof-law, on the river Sana, the third of June 1714, and promised him powerful succours. War was now declared against the Turks, in the name of these two monarchs; but the Polish diet, not willing to break with the Ottoman Porte, refused to ratify the engagement their king had entered into. It was the fate of the Czar to have an impotent ally ly in king Augustus. He entertained the same hopes of assistance from the princes of Moldavia and Walachia, and, in like manner, met with the same disappointments.

These two provinces ought to have taken this opportunity to shake off the Turkish yoke. These countries were those of the ancient Daci, who, together with the Gepidi, with whom they were intermixed, did, for a long time, disturb the Roman empire. They were subdued by the emperor Trajan, and Constantine the Great converted them to the Christian religion. Dacia was one of the provinces of the eastern empire, but shortly after, these very people contributed to the subversion of the west, by serving in the armies of Odoacer and Theodoric.

These countries were afterwards subject to the Greek empire, and when the Turks made themselves masters of Constantinople, were governed and oppressed by particular princes; at length, they were totally subjected by the Padicha or Turkish emperor, who now granted them in investiture. The Hospodar or Vaivod, chosen by the Ottoman Porte to govern these provinces, is always a Christian of the Greek church. The Turks, by this choice, gave a proof of their toleration, while our ignorant declaimers are accusing them of persecution. The prince who has this office is tributary to, or rather farms these countries of the Grand Signior; this dignity being always given to the best bidder, or him who makes the greatest presents to the grand vizir, in the same manner as the office of Greek patriarch at Constantinople.

stantinople. Sometimes this government is bestowed on a dragoman, that is, by an interpreter of the divan. These provinces are seldom under the government of the same vaivod, the Porte chusing to divide them, in order to secure their obedience. Demetrius Cantemir was at this time vaivod of Moldavia. This prince was said to be descended from Tamerlane, because Tamerlane's true name was *Timur*, and Timur was a Tartarian khan; and so, from the name *Tamurkan*, say they, came the family of *Kantemir*.

BASSARABA Branconan had been invested with the principality of Walachia, but had not found any genealogist to make him the descendant of a Tartarian conqueror. Cantemir thought this a proper time to shake off the Turkish yoke, and render himself independent by means of the Czar's protection. He acted in the very same manner with Peter as Mazeppa had done with Charles XII. He even engaged Bassaraba for the present to join him in the conspiracy, of which he hoped to reap all the benefit himself; his design being to seize the sovereignty of both provinces. The bishop of Jerusalem, who was at that time at Walachia, was the soul of this conspiracy. Cantemir promised the Czar to furnish him with men and provisions, as Mazeppa did the king of Sweden, and kept his word no better than he had done.

GENERAL Scheremetow advanced, as far as Jassi, the capital of Moldavia, to reconnoitre the country, and assist in the execution of these great projects. Cantemir came thither to meet him, and was received

ceived with all the honours due to a prince: but the only princely action he did was that of publishing a manifesto against the Turkish empire. The hospodar of Walachia, who soon discovered the ambitious views of his collegue, quitted his party, and returned to his duty. The bishop of Jerusalem justly dreading the punishment due to his perfidy, fled and concealed himself: the people of Walachia and Moldavia continued faithful to the Grand Signior, and those who were to have supplied provisions for the Russian army, carried them to the Turks.

The vizir Baltagi Mehemet had already crossed the Danube at the head of one hundred thousand men, and was directing his march towards Jassi, along the banks of the river Pruth (formerly the Hierasus) which runs into the Danube, and which nearly makes the boundary of Moldavia and Bassarabia. He then dispatched count Poniatowski, a Polish gentleman, attached to the fortunes of the king of Sweden, to desire that prince to make him a visit and see his army. Charles would not consent to this proposal: he insisted, that the grand vizir should make him the first visit, in the asylum near Bender. When Poniatowsky returned to the Ottoman camp, and endeavoured to excuse this refusal of his master, the vizir, turning to the khan of the Tartars, said, "This is what I expected from this proud Pagan." This mutual pride, which never fails of alienating the minds of those in power from each other, did no service to the king of Sweden; and indeed that prince ought to have

seen

seen from the beginning, that the Turks act for their own interest.

WHILE the Turkish army was passing the Danube, the Czar advanced by the frontiers of Poland, and passed the Boristhenes, in order to extricate Marshal Scheremetow, who was then on the banks of the Pruth, to the southward of Jassi, and in danger of being daily surrounded by an army of one hundred thousand Turks, and an army of Tartars. The Czar, before he passed the Boristhenes, was in doubt whether he should expose his beloved Catherine to these dangers which seemed to encrease every day; but Catherine, on her side, looked upon this solicitude of the Czar for her ease and safety, as an affront offered to her affection and courage, and pressed him so strongly on this head, that he could not but consent that she should pass the river with him. The soldiers beheld her with joy and admiration, marching on horseback at the head of the troops, for she rarely made use of a carriage. After passing the Boristhenes, they had a tract of desert country to pass through, and then to cross the Bog, and afterwards the river Tiras, now called the Neister, after which they had another desert to traverse, before they came to the banks of the Pruth. Catherine, during this fatiguing march, animated the whole army by her chearfulness and affability. She sent refreshments to such of the officers who were sick, and extended her care even to the common soldiers.

THEY at length arrived at Jassi †. Here he was

† July 4. 1711.

to establish his magazine. Bassaraba, the hospodar of Walachia, who had again embraced the interest of the Ottoman Porte, but still, in appearance, continued a friend to the Czar, promised to this prince to make peace with the Turks, although the grand vizir had given him no such commission. The Czar contented himself with demanding only provisions for his army, which Bassaraba neither would nor could furnish. It was very difficult to procure any supplies from Poland; and these, which prince Cantemir had promised, and which he vainly hoped from Walachia, was not possible to be brought from thence. These disappointments rendered the situation of the Russians extremely critical; and to add to their afflictions, they were tormented with prodigious swarms of locusts, which devoured the whole produce of the country, and filled the air with their stench. They were so distressed for want of water, that they were obliged to bring it in casks to supply the camp, from a considerable distance.

During this dangerous and fatiguing march, the Czar, by a singular fatality, found himself at a small distance from his rival Charles, Bender not being above twenty-five leagues from the place where the Russian army was encamped near Jassi. Some parties of Cossacks made excursions even to the place of Charles's retreat; but the Crim Tartars, who hovered round that part of the country, sufficiently secured him from any surprise; and Charles waited in his camp, with an undaunted impatience, the issue of the war.

PETER

PETER no sooner had established some magazines than he marched in haste with his army to the right of the river Pruth. His chief object was to prevent the Turks, who were posted to the left, and towards the head of the river, from crossing it, and marching towards him. This effected, he would then be master of Moldavia and Walachia. With this view he dispatched general Janus with the van-guard of the army, to oppose the passage of the Turks; but the general did not arrive till they had already begun to cross the river upon their bridges; upon which he was obliged to retreat, and his infantry was closely pursued by the Turks, till the Czar came up in person to his assistance, and extricated him from the Turks.

THE grand vizir now marched directly along the river towards the Czar. The two armies were very unequal in point of number: that of the Turks, which had been reinforced by the Tartarian troops, consisted of near two hundred and fifty thousand men, while that of the Russians hardly amounted to thirty seven thousand. There was indeed a considerable body of troops, headed by general Renne, on their march from the other side of the Moldavian mountains; but the Turks had cut off all communication with these parts.

THE Czar's army now began to be in want of provisions, nor could, without the greatest difficulty, procure water, though encamped at no great distance from the river, being exposed to a furious discharge of the numerous artillery which the grand
vizir

vizir had caused to be planted on the left side of the river, under the care of a body of troops that kept up a constant fire against the Russians. By this relation, which may be depended upon for a truth, Baltagi Mehemet, the Turkish vizir, far from being the pusillanimous or weak commander which the Swedes have represented him, gave proofs on this occasion that he perfectly well understood his business. The passing the Pruth in the sight of the enemy, obliging him to retreat; the cutting off all communication between the Czar's army, and a body of cavalry that was marching to reinforce it, the hemming in his army, without the least probability of a retreat, and the cutting off all supplies of water and provisions, by keeping it constantly under the check of the batteries on the opposite side of the river, were manœuvres that shewed him to be an experienced and wise general.

PETER now saw himself in a more critical situation than that to which he had reduced his rival Charles XII. at Pultowa, being, like him, surrounded by a superior army, and in greater want of provisions, and, like him, having confided in the promises of a prince too powerful to be bound by those promises; he resolved upon a retreat, and endeavoured to return towards Jassi in order to chuse a more advantageous situation for his camp.

FOR this purpose he decamped under favour of the night *; but his army had scarcely begun its

* July 20. 1711.

march, when, at break of day, the Turks fell upon his rear; but the Preobrafinſki regiment falling about, and ſtanding firm, did, for a conſiderable time, check the fury of their onſet. The Ruſſians then formed themſelves, and made a line of entrenchments with their waggons and baggage. The ſame day the Turks returned again to the attack with the whole body of their army; and as a proof that the Ruſſians knew how to defend themſelves, let what will be alledged to the contrary, they alſo made head againſt this very ſuperior force for a conſiderable time, killed a great number of their enemies, without being thrown into confuſion, though they uſed all their endeavours to break in upon them †.

THERE were in the Ottoman army two officers belonging to Charles XII. namely, count Poniatowſki, and the count of Spare, who had the command of a body of Coſſacks in that prince's intereſt. My memorials ſay, that theſe generals adviſed the grand vizir not to fight with the Ruſſians, and content himſelf with depriving them of ſupplies of water and proviſions, which would oblige them either to ſurrender priſoners of war, or to periſh: other accounts pretend, on the contrary, that theſe officers would have perſuaded the grand vizir to fall upon this feeble and half-ſtarved army, in a weak and diſtreſſed condition, and put all to the ſword. The firſt of theſe ſeems to be the moſt prudent and circumſpect; but the

† July 21.

VOL. II. B ſecond

second is more agreeable to generals bred under Charles XII.

The real fact is, that the grand vizir fell upon the rear of the Russian army at day-break, which was thrown into confusion, and there remained only a line of four hundred men to confront the Turks. This small body formed itself with amazing quickness, under the orders of a German general named Alard, who, to his immortal honour, made such a rapid and excellent disposition on this occasion, that the Russians withstood, for upwards of three hours, the repeated attack of the whole Ottoman army, without losing ground.

The Czar now found himself amply repaid for the immense pains he had taken to habituate his troops to strict discipline. At the battle of Narva, sixty thousand men were defeated by only eight thousand, because the former were undisciplined; and here we see a rear-guard of eight thousand Russians, sustaining the efforts of one hundred and fifty thousand Turks, killing seven thousand of them, and forcing the rest to return back.

After this sharp engagement, the two armies entrenched themselves for that night: but the Russians remained enclosed, and deprived of all provisions, even of water; for notwithstanding they were so near the river Pruth, yet they did not dare approach its banks; for as soon as any soldiers went out to seek water, a body of Turks posted on the opposite side of the river drove them back by a furious discharge from their cannon loaded with chain shot: and the body of the Turkish army

army which had attacked the Ruffians, continued to fire upon them from another quarter with all their artillery.

The Ruffian army appeared to be now quite undone, by its pofition, the inequality of numbers, and the want of provifions. The fkirmifhes of both fides were frequent and bloody: the Ruffian cavalry being almoft all difmounted, could no longer be of any affiance, unlefs by fighting on foot: in fine, the fituation of affairs was defperate. It was out of their power to retreat, they had nothing left but to gain a compleat victory, to perifh to the laft man, or to be made flaves by the infidels.

All the accounts and memoirs of thefe times unanimoufly agree, that the Czar, divided within himfelf, whether or not he fhould expofe his wife, his army, his empire, and the fruits of all his labours, to almoft inevitable deftruction; retired to his tent overwhelmed with grief, and agitated with violent convulfions, to which he was naturally fubject, and which the prefent bad fituation of his affairs redoubled on him. In this condition he remained alone, a prey to fo many cruel inquietudes; not wanting that any body fhould be witnefs to his diftracted condition, he forbid any perfon to enter his tent. But Catherine hearing of his diforders, forced her way into him, and on this occafion Peter found how happy it was for him that he had permitted his wife to follow him in this expedition.

A wife who like her had faced death in all
thofe

these combats, and had exposed her person, like a common soldier, to the fire of the Turkish artillery, for the sake of her husband, had an unboubted right to speak to her husband, and to be heard. The Czar accordingly listened to what she had to say, and in the end suffered himself to be persuaded to try and send to the vizir with proposals for a truce.

It has been a custom throughout the east, that when any person demands an audience of the sovereign or his representative, they must not presume to come near them without a present. On this occasion therefore Catherine collected together the few precious stones which she had brought with her, on this military tour, in which no magnificence or luxury were admitted; to these she added the furs of two black foxes, and what ready money she could collect; the latter was designed for a present to the kiaja. She made choice herself of an officer, in whose fidelity and understanding she thought she could depend, who, accompanied with two servants, was to carry the presents to the grand vizir, and afterwards to deliver the money intended for the kiaja into his own hand. The officer was charged with a letter from marshal Scheremetow to Mehemet. The memoirs of Czar Peter mention this letter, but they say nothing of the other particulars of Catherine's conduct in this business; however, they are sufficiently confirmed by the declaration of Peter himself in 723, when he caused Catherine to be crowned empress, wherein we find these words; "She has been of the greatest

greatest use to us in all our dangers, and particularly at the battle of Pruth, when our army was reduced to twenty two thousand men." If the Czar had then indeed no more men capable of bearing arms, the service which Catherine did him on that occasion, was fully equivalent to the honours and dignities conferred upon her. The MS. journal of Peter the Great says, that the day of the battle, on the twentieth of July, he had thirty one thousand five hundred and fifty four infantry, and six thousand six hundred and ninety two cavalry, the latter almost all dismounted; he must then have lost sixteen thousand two hundred and forty six men in that engagement. The same memoirs assure, that the loss sustained by the Turks was more considerable than that of the Russians; for attacking them in crouds, and without any order, every shot had its desired effect. If this is fact, the battle of the twentieth or twenty-first of July has been one of the most bloody that had been known for several ages.

We must either suspect Peter the Great of having been mistaken, in his declaration at the crowning of the empress, when he acknowledges " his obligations to her for having saved his army, which was reduced to twenty-two thousand men;" or deny the truth of his journal, wherein he affirms, that the day on which the above battle was fought, his army, exclusive of the succours he expected from the other side of the Moldavian mountains, amounted to thirty-one thousand five hundred and fifty-four foot, and six thousand six hundred and

B 3 ninety-

ninety-two horse. According to this calculation, the battle of Pruth must have been by far more terrible and bloody than the historians or memorialists have represented on either side. There must certainly be some mistake here, a thing very common in the relations of campaigns, especially, when the author enters into a minute relation of circumstances. The surest method therefore on these occasions, is to confine ourselves to the principal events, the victory, and the defeat; as we can but seldom know with certainty the exact loss on either side.

WHATEVER might be the reduction of the Russian army, there were still hopes that the grand vizir, deceived by their obstinate resistance, might be induced to grant them peace upon such terms as might be honourable to the Porte, and at the same time not absolutely disgraceful to those of the empire of Russia. It was the great merit of Catherine to have perceived this possibility, at a time when the Czar and his generals saw nothing but inevitable destruction.

NORBERG, in his history of Charles XII quotes a letter, sent by the Czar to the grand vizir, in which he expresses himself thus. "If, contrary to my intentions, I have been so unhappy as to incur the displeasure of his highness, I am ready to make reparation for any cause of complaint he may have against me. I conjure you, most noble general, to prevent the further effusion of blood; give orders, I beseech you, to put a stop to the dreadful and destructive

ſtructive fire of your artillery, and accept of the hoſtage I herewith ſend you."

THIS letter carries all the marks of falſity with it, as do indeed moſt of the random pieces of Norberg. It is dated eleventh of July, N S. whereas no letter was ſent to Baltagi Mehemet, till the twenty-firſt, N. S. neither was it the Czar that wrote to the vizir, but his general Scheremetow: there were no ſuch expreſſions made uſe of as "if the Czar has had the misfortune to incur the diſpleaſure of his highneſs," ſuch terms as theſe being ſuitable only to a ſubject who implores the pardon of his ſovereign, whom he has offended. There was no mention made of any hoſtage, nor was any one ſent. The letter was carried by an officer, in the midſt of a furious connonade on both ſides. Scheremetow in this letter only reminded the vizir of certain overtures of peace, that the Porte had made at the beginning of the campaign through the mediation of the Dutch and Engliſh miniſters, and by which the divan demanded that the fort and harbour of Taganroc ſhould be given up, which were the real objects of the war.

SOME hours elapſed before the meſſenger received an anſwer from the grand vizir*, and it was apprehended that he had either been killed by the enemy's cannon, or that they had detained him priſoner. A ſecond courier was therefore diſpatched with a duplicate of the former letter, and a council

* July 21. 1711.

of war immediately held, at which Catherine was prefent. At this council ten general officers figned the following refolution.

"Resolved, if the enemy will not accept the conditions propofed, and fhould infift upon laying down our arms, and furrendering at difcretion, that all the minifters and general officers are unanimoufly of opinion, to cut their way through the enemy fword in hand."

In confequence of this refolution, a line of entrenchments was thrown round the baggage, and the Ruffians marched fome few paces out of their camp, towards the enemy, when the grand vizir caufed a fufpenfion of arms to be proclaimed between the two armies.

All the writers of the Swedifh party have treated the grand vizir as a cowardly and traiterous wretch, who had been bribed to fell the honour of his mafter's arms. In the fame manner many writers have accufed count Piper of receiving money from the duke of Marlborough, to perfuade the king of Sweden to continue the war againft the Czar; and the French minifter has been charged with purchafing the peace of Seville for a ftipulated fum. Such accufations ought never to be advanced but on very ftrong proofs. It is very feldom that a prime minifter will ftoop to fuch meanneffes, which are always difcovered fooner or later by thofe who pay the money, or by the treafury accounts, which never lie. A minifter of ftate has the eyes of the whole world on his actions. His credit and influence depend wholly upon his character, and he

is

is generally so rich as to be above the temptation of a bribe.

The part of viceroy of the Turkish empire is so illustrious, and the profits annexed to it, in time of war, so immense; there was such a profusion of every thing in the camp of Baltagi Mehemet, and, on the other hand, so much poverty and distress in that of the Czar, that surely the grand vizir was rather in a condition to give than to receive. The small present of a woman who had nothing to send but a few skins and some precious stones, in compliance with the established custom of all courts, or rather those in particular of the east, can never be looked upon as bribery. The frank and open conduct of Baltagi Mehemet seems at once to give the lie to the black accusation with which so many writers have stained their relations. Vice-chancellor Shaffiroff paid the vizir a public visit in his tent: every thing was transacted in this open manner on both sides; and indeed it could not be otherwise. The very negotiation was entered upon in the presence of a person in the service of the king of Sweden, a domestick of count Poniatowski, who was himself one of that monarch's generals. This man served as interpreter, and the several articles were publicly taken down in writing by the vizir's chief secretary, Hammer Effendi. Moreover, count Poniatowski was there in person. The present sent to the kiaja was offered probably in form, and every thing was transacted according to the oriental manner. Other presents were made by the Turks in return; so that there was

was not the least appearance of treachery. - The motives which determined the vizir to consent to the proposals offered him, were, first, that the body of troops under the command of general Renne, on the borders of the river Sireth, in Moldavia, had already crossed three rivers, and were actually in the neighbourhood of the Danube, where Renne had already made himself master of the town and castle of Brahila, defended by a numerous garrison, under the command of a bashaw. Secondly, the Czar had likewise another body of troops advancing through the frontiers of Poland; and, lastly, it is more than probable that the vizir was not fully acquainted with the extreme want that was felt in the Russian camp. One enemy always hides from another an exact account of his provisions and ammunition; on the contrary, either side are accustomed rather to make a boast of plenty, even in a time when they are in the greatest wants. There can be no other artifices practised to gain intelligence of the true state of an adversary's affairs, by means of spies, between the Turks and Russians. The difference of their dress, of their religion, and of their language will not permit. They are moreover strangers to that desertion which prevails in most of our armies, and consequently the grand vizir could not know the desperate condition of the Czar's army.

BALTAGI, who was not fond of war, and who, nevertheless, had conducted this very well, thought that his expedition would be sufficiently successful if he could deliver to the Grand Seignior the towns and

and harbours fo which he was fighting, ftop the progrefs of the victorious army un ler Renne, and obliging that general to quit the banks of the Danube, return back into Ruffia and for ever fhut the entrance of the Palus Mæotis, the Cimmerian Bofphorus, and the Black Sea, againft the enterprifing prince; and, laftly, if he avoided taking thefe certain advantages, on the hazard of a new battle, in which, after all, defpair might have got the better of fuperiority of numbers. The preceding day only, he had obferved his Janiffaries repulfed with lofs; and there wanted not examples of many victories being gained by the fmaller army over the greater. Such were Mehemet's reafons for accepting the propofals of peace. His conduct, however, did not merit the approbation of Charles's officers, who ferved in the Turkifh army, nor of the khan of Tartary. It was the intereft of the latter, and his followers, to reject all terms of accommodation which would deprive them of the opportunity of ravaging the frontiers of Ruffia and Poland. Charles XII defired to be revenged on his rival the Czar; but the general, and the firft minifter of the Ottoman empire, was neither animated by thirft of revenge, which animated Charles XII. nor by the defire of booty, which fwayed the Tartar chief.

As foon as the fufpenfion of arms was agreed on; and figned, the Ruffians purchafed the provifions of the Turks, of which they ftood in need. The articles of peace were not figned at that time, as is related by La Motraye, and which Norberg has

B 6   copied

copied from him. The vizir, among other conditions, demanded that the Czar should not concern himself any more in the Polish affairs. This was a point particularly infisted upon by count Poniatowski; but it was, in fact, the interest of the Ottoman crown, that the kingdom of Poland should continue in its then defenceless and divided state; accordingly this demand was reduced to that of the Russian troops evacuating the frontiers of Poland. The khan of Tartary, on his side, demanded a tribute of forty thousand sequins. This point, after being long debated, was not agreed to.

THE grand vizir infisted a long time, that prince Cantemir should be delivered up to him, as Patkul had been to the king of Sweden. Cantemir was exactly in the same situation as Mazeppa had been. The Czar had caused that hetman to be arraigned and tried for his defection, and afterwards to be executed in effigy. The Turks were not acquainted with the nature of such proceeding; they knew nothing of trials for contumacy, nor of publick condemnations. The affixing a fentence on any perfon, and executing him in effigy, were not known among them, as their law forbids the reprefentation of any human likeness whatever. The vizir in vain insisted on Cantemir's being delivered up; Peter peremptorily refused to comply, and wrote the following letter with his own hand, to his vice-chancellor Shaffiroff.

"I CAN resign to the Turks all the country as far as Curzka, because I have hopes of being able to recover it again; but I will, by no means, violate

late my faith, which, once forfeited, can never be retrieved I have nothing I can properly call my own, but my honour. It I give up that, I cease to be longer a king."

At length the treaty was concluded, and signed, near a village called Falkfen, on the river Pruth. Among other things, it was stipulated, that Afoph, and the territories belonging thereto, should be restored, together with all the ammunition and artillery that were in the place, before the Czar made himself master thereof, in 1690. That the harbour of Taganroc, in the Zabach Sea, should be demolished, as also that of Samara, on the river of the same name; and several other fortresses. There was likewise another article added, respecting the king of Sweden, which plainly shews the displeasure the vizir had for that prince; for it was therein stipulated, that the Czar should not molest Charles in his return to his dominions, and that afterwards the Czar and he might make peace with each other, if they were so disposed.

By the wording of this extraordinary article, it is evident, that Baltagi Mehemet had not forgot the haughty manner in which Charles XII had behaved to him a little time before; and it is not unlikely that this very behaviour of the king of Sweden might have been one reason why Mehemet so readily complied with his rival's proposals for peace. Charles's glory depended wholly on the ruin of the Czar; but we are seldom inclinable to praise those who express a contempt for us: however, this prince, who refused, when invited, to pay the

the vizir a vifit in his camp, when it was certainly his intereſt to have been in friendſhip with him, now came in great haſte, and unaſked, when the work that put an end to all his hopes was on the point of being concluded. The vizir did not go to meet him in perſon, but contented himſelf with ſending two of his baſhaws, deferring that ceremony till Charles was near his tent.

THIS interview was taken up with mutual reproaches. It has been thought that the anſwer which the vizir made to Charles, when that prince reproached him with not making the Czar priſoner, when he might have done it ſo eaſily, was the reply of a weak man. "I I had taken him priſoner, ſaid Mehemet, who would have governed his empire?"

IT is very eaſy however to ſee, that this was the anſwer of a man who had been affronted; and theſe words which he added, "for it is not proper that every king ſhould leave his dominions," ſufficiently ſhews his deſign to mortify the hoſt of Bender.

CHARLES gained nothing by his journey, but the pleaſure of tearing the vizir's robe with one of his ſpurs, while that officer, who might have made him repent this inſult, took no notice of it, by which he ſhewed himſelf greatly ſuperior to Charles. If any thing could have made that monarch ſenſible in the midſt of his life, how eaſily fortune can put greatneſs to the bluſh, it would have been the reflection, that at the battle of Pultowa a paltry-cook's boy had obliged the whole army to ſurrender

at

at difcretion, and in this of Pruth a wood cutter was the arbiter of his fate, and that of his rival the Czar; for the vizir Baltagi Mehemet had been a cutter of wood in the Grand Seignior's feraglio, as his name implied; and far from being afhamed of that title, he accounted it an honour: fo very different are the manners of the eaftern people from ours.

WHEN the account of this treaty came to Conftantinople, the fultan was fo well fatisfied, that he ordered public rejoicings to be made for a whole week, and Mehemet's kiaja, who brought the news to the divan, was inftantly raifed to the dignity of Boujouk Imraour, or mafter of the horfe; a fure proof that the fultan did not think his vizir guilty of cowardice.

NORBERG feems to have known very little of the Tuikifh government, when he fays, that " the Grand Seignior was obliged to keep in friendfhip with Baltagi Mehemet, that vizir having rendered himfelf powerful" The Janiffaries indeed have often rendered themfelves formidable to their fultans; but there is not a fingle example of a vizir who has not been readily facrificed when ordered for execution by the fultan, and Mehemet was not able to fupport himfelf by his own power. Befides, Norberg manifeftly contradicts himfelf, by affirming in the fame page, that the Janiffaries were provoked againft Mehemet, and that the fultan was afraid of his power.

THE king of Sweden was now reduced to the mean fhift of forming cabals in the Ottoman court; and

and a monarch who had so lately made kings by his own power, was now seen waiting for audience, and offering memorials and petitions which were refused.

CHARLES ran through all the ambages of intrigue, like a subject who endeavours to make a minister suspected by his master. In this manner he acted against Mehemet, and against those who succeeded him. Sometimes application was made to the sultana Valide by means of a Jewess, who had admission into the seraglio; at other times, he bribed one of the eunuchs for the same purpose. At length he formed a scheme for a man to pass among the Grand Seignior's guards, and, by counterfeiting madness, to be taken notice of by the sultan, and by that means deliver up into his own hand a memorial for Charles. All these different schemes had only the effect of depriving him of his daily pension of one thousand five hundred French livres a day *. At the same time the grand vizir, in a friendly manner, advised him to quit the Grand Seignior's dominions.

CHARLES, however, was resolved not to depart, buoying up himself with vain hopes, that he should once more re-enter Poland and Russia with a powerful army of Turks. All the world knows what was the end of this foolish boldness in the year 1714, and how he engaged an army of Janissaries, Spahis and Tartars, with only himself, his secretaries, and his valet de chambre, cook and stable-

* About seventy pounds sterling.

men; that he was made prisoner in that country, where he had been used with the greatest hospitality; and that he made his escape back to his own kingdom in the disguise of a courier, after having lived five years in Turky. Now it must be owned, if there was any rationality in his conduct, it is quite different from the conduct of every rational man.

CHAP. II.

Conclusion of the affairs of Pruth.

TO give a perfect account of this it will be necessary to repeat an event already related in the history of Charles XII It happened during the suspension of arms before the treaty of Pruth, that two Tartarian soldiers took prisoners two Italian officers belonging to the Czar's army, and offered them to sale to an officer of the Janissaries. The vizir being informed of this breach of public faith, ordered them to be put to death How are we to reconcile this rigid punctuality with the violation of the law of nations in the person of Tolstoy the Czar's ambassador, whom this same vizir caused to be seized in the streets of Constantinople, and thrown into prison? There is always some reason for the contradictions we find in the actions of mankind.
Baltagi

Baltagi Mehemet was displeased with the khan of the Tartars, for having opposed the peace he had lately made, and was resolved to let him know that he was his master.

The treaty being signed, the Czar left the borders of the Pruth, returned back to his own dominions, followed by eight thousand Turks, whom the vizir had sent as an army of observation to watch the motions of the Russians, and also to serve as an escort for them against the insults of the ravaging Tartars.

Peter, agreeable to the treaty, gave orders to demolish the fortresses of Samara and Kamienska; but the restoring of Asoph, and the demolition of the port of Taganroc, met with more difficulty in the execution. By the terms of the treaty it was necessary to distinguish the artillery and ammunitions which belonged to the Turks in Asoph before that place was taken by the Czar, from those that had been sent thither after it fell into his hands. The governor was very dilatory, at which the Porte was greatly inraged, and not without reason The sultan was impatient to received the keys of Asoph: the vizir promised they should be sent from time to time, but the governor always found means to delay the giving them up. Baltagi Mehemet lost the favour of his master, and with it his post. The khan of the Tartars, and his other enemies, prevailed against him with the sultan: this involved him in disgrace, with several other bashaws; but the Grand Seignior, being fully convinced of his honesty, did not deprive him either of his life or estate,

state, but sent him to Mytilene, as governor [*].
This simple removal from the helm of affairs, and
the continuing to him his fortunes, and above all,
the giving him the command in Mytilene, sufficiently contradicts all that Norberg has advanced to
make us believe that this vizir had been bribed by
Peter.

NORBERG further says, that the Bostangi bashaw, who acquainted him with his disgrace, declared him at the same time, "a traitor, that had
disobeyed the orders of the Grand Seignior, had
sold himself to the enemy for money, and was found
guilty of having neglected the interests of the king
of Sweden." In the first place, these kind of declarations are never used in Turky; the orders
of the Grand Seignior always being issued privately,
and executed with secrecy. Secondly, if the vizir
had been declared *a traitor, a rebel, and a corrupted person*, crimes of this nature, in a country where
they are never forgiven, would have been immediately punished with death. Lastly, if he had
been criminal for not attending to the interests of
the king of Sweden, it is plain that this prince
must have had so much influence at the Ottoman
Porte, as to have made the other ministers to
tremble, who would by all means have endeavoured to gain his good graces; whereas, on the contrary, the bashaw Jussuf, aga of the Janissaries,
who succeeded Mehemet Baltagi as grand vizir,
was of the same opinion as his predecessor, in rela-

[*] Nov. 1711.

tion to the conduct of Charles XII. and was so far from doing him any service, that he used all possible means to get rid of so dangerous a guest; and when count Poniatowski, the companion and confident of that monarch, went to compliment the vizir on his new dignity, the latter said thus to him: "Mind, I forewarn thee, infidel, that if ever I find thee caballing, I will upon the first notice cause thee to be thrown into the sea with a stone about thy neck."

This compliment Poniatowski himself relates in the memoirs he drew up at my desire, which is a sufficient proof of the little influence his master had in the Turkish court. All that Norberg has related with regard to the affairs of that empire, plainly appears to come from a prejudiced person, and one who wanted proper information of the circumstances of things he pretends to write about. And we may count among the errors of a party spirit, and political falshoods, every thing which this writer advances unsupported by proofs, concerning the corruption of a grand vizir, that is, of a man who had the disposal of above sixty millions per annum, without being subject to the least account. I have now before me the letter that count Poniatowski wrote to king Stanislaus immediately after the signing the treaty of Pruth, in which he upbraids Baltagi Mehemet with the slight he shewed to the king of Sweden, his dislike to the war, and unsteadiness of his temper; but never once hints the least charge of corruption; for he knew too well what the place of grand vizir was, to think

that

that the Czar was capable of setting a price upon the infidelity of the second person in the Ottoman empire

SHAFFIROFF and Scheremetow, who remained at Constantinople as hostages on the part of the Czar for his performance of the treaty, were not used in the manner they would have been, if known to have purchased this peace, and to have acted in concert with the vizir in deceiving his master. They were left to go at liberty about the city, and had two companies of Janissaries to protect them.

TOLSTOY, the Czar's ambassador, having been released from his imprisonment in the Seven Towers, immediately upon signing the treaty of Pruth, the Dutch and English ambassadors engaged with the new vizir to see the several articles of the treaty performed.

ASOPH was at last restored to the Turks, and the fortresses mentioned in the treaty were demolished according to stipulation. And now the Ottoman Porte, though very little inclinable to interfere in the differences between Christian princes, could not without vanity behold itself made arbitrator between Russia, Poland, and the king of Sweden; the Grand Seignior insisted that the Czar should withdraw his troops out of Poland, and free the Turkish empire from so dangerous a neighbour; and desirous that the Christian princes might continually be at war with each other, desired nothing so much as to send Charles home to his own dominions; but would never fur-

nish

nish him with an army. The Tartars were always for war, as being a lucrative trade. The Janissaries wished for it, but more out of hatred against the Christians, their natural ferocity, and from a love of rapine and licentiousness, than from any other motives. Nevertheless, the English and Dutch ministers managed their negotiations so well, that they prevailed over the opposite party; the treaty of Pruth was confirmed, but with the addition of a new article, by which it was stipulated, that the Czar should withdraw his forces from Poland within three months, and that the sultan should immediately send Charles XII. out of his dominions.

This treaty plainly shews the interest the king of Sweden had at the Porte. He was evidently sacrificed on this occasion by the new vizir bashaw Jussuf, as he had been before by Baltagi Mehemet. Those historians who have wrote in his favour can find nothing to apologize for this fresh affront, but that of accusing Jussuf, of having been bribed as well as his predecessor. Such repeated assertions, unsupported by any proofs, are rather the clamours of an impotent cabal, than the testimonies of history. But faction, when driven to acknowledge facts, will ever be endeavouring to alter circumstances and motives, and unhappily it is thus that all the histories of our times will be handed down to posterity, so altered, that they will be scarcely able to distinguish the truth.

CHAP.

CHAP. III.

Marriage of the Czarowitz ; and solemn declaration of Peter's marriage with Catherine. Her brother makes himself known.

THIS misfortunate campaign of the Pruth was more fatal to the Czar than the battle of Narva had been; for after that defeat he had found means not only to retrieve his losses, but also to dispossess Charles XII. of Ingria; but by the treaty of Falkilen, in which he consented to give up to the sultan his forts and harbours on the Palus Mæotis, he for ever lost his projected superiority in the Black Sea. His enterprises afforded him a large field for action ; his new establishments in Russia were to be compleated, he had to prosecute his victories over the Swedes, to re-establish king Augustus on the Polish throne, and to cement properly his alliance with the several powers; but the fatigues he hath undergone having impaired his health, he was obliged to go to Carelsbed in Bohemia, to drink the waters of that place. While he was there, he gave orders for his troops to enter Pomerania, who blockaded Stralsund, and took five other towns.

POMERANIA is the most northern provine of Germany, bounded on the east by Prussia and Poland,

land, on the west by Brandenburg, on the south by Mecklenburg, and on the north by the Baltic Sea. It has had different masters almost every century: Gustavus Adolphus took possession of it in his famous war of thirty years, and it was afterwards solemnly given up to the Swedes, by the treaty of Westphalia, with a reservation of the bishoprick of Camin, and some other small places lying in Upper Pomerania. The whole of this province properly belongs to the elector of Brandenburg, in virtue of a family agreement made with the dukes of Pomerania, whose family being extinct in 1637, consequently by the laws of the empire the house of Brandenburg had an undoubted right to the succession: but necessity, the primary law, occasioned this family compact to be set aside by the treaty of Osnaburg: after which almost the whole of Pomerania fell to the lot of the victorious Swedes.

The Czar's scheme was to take from Sweden all the provinces that crown was possessed of in Germany; and, in order to accomplish his design, he found it necessary to enter into an alliance with the electors of Hanover and Brandenburg, and the king of Denmark. Peter drew up the several articles of the treaty he designed with these powers, and also a perfect account of the necessary operations for rendering him master of Pomerania.

In the mean time he went to Torgou to be present at the nuptials of his son the Czarowitz Alexis

lexis with the princess of Wolfenbuttel ‡, sister to the consort of Charles VI emperor of Germany; nuptials, which in the end destroyed his own peace of mind, and both the parties afterwards fell a sacrifice to it.

The Czarowitz was a son of the first marriage of Peter the Great with Eudocia Lapoukin, to whom he was espoused in 1689: she was at this time shut up in the monastery of Susdal; their son Alexis Petrowitz, who was born the 1st of March 1690, was now in his 22d year. This prince was not then at all known in Europe: a minister, whose memoirs of the court of Russia have been printed, says, in a letter he writes to his master, dated August 25, 1711, that " this prince was tall and well-made, resembled his father greatly, was of an excellent disposition, very pious, had read the bible five times over, took great delight in the ancient Greek historians, appeared to have a very quick apprehension and understanding, was well acquainted with the mathematics, the art of war, navigation, hydraulics; that he understood the German language, and was then learning the French, but that his father would never suffer him to go through a regular course of study fit for a gentleman.

The Czar himself gave a quite different character of his son than this, in which we shall see with how much grief he reproaches him with faults quite opposite to those good qualities which this minister seems so much to admire him for.

‡ Oct. 23. 1711.

POSTERITY muſt therefore determine between the teſtimony of a ſtranger, who may have formed too ſlight a judgment, and the declaration of a parent, who thought it his duty to ſacrifice the dictates of nature to the good of his people. If the miniſter was no better acquainted with the diſpoſition of Alexis's mind than the form of his body, his evidence will have no weight; for he deſcribes this prince as tall and well made, whereas the memoirs ſent me from Peterſburg ſay that he was neither.

CATHERINE, his mother in law, was not preſent at the marriage; for though ſhe was already looked upon as Czarina, yet ſhe had not been publicly acknowledged as ſuch; and moreover, having only the title of highneſs given her at the Czar's court, her rank was not ſufficiently known to admit of her ſigning the-contract, or to appear at the ceremony in a ſtation befitting the ſpouſe of Peter the Great. She therefore remained at Thorn in Poliſh Pruſſia The Czar immediately ſent the new-married couple away to Wolfenbuttel ¶, and brought back Catherine to Peterſburg with the ſame expedition he was ſo much famed for.

AFTER marrying his ſon †, he gave orders for the public ſolemnizing his own nuptials with Catherine, which had been declared in private before. The ceremony was performed with as much ſplendor as could be expected in a city but yet in its infancy, and from finances, drained by the late deſtructive war with the Turks, and that which he

¶ Jan. 9. 1712. † Feb. 19.

was

was still engaged in against the king of Sweden. The Czar gave directions for, and assisted in, all the preparations for the ceremony, according to his usual custom; and Catherine was now publicly declared Czarina, as a reward for having saved her husband and his army.

The acclamations with which this declaration was received at Petersburg were sincere: the applauses which subjects confer upon the actions of a despotic sovereign are sometimes suspected; but on this occasion they were confirmed by the united voice of all the thinking part of Europe, who saw with pleasure on the one hand the heir of a vast Monarchy with no other glory than that of his birth, married to a petty princess; and, on the other hand, a powerful conqueror, and a law-giver, publicly sharing his bed and his throne with a stranger and a captive, who had only merit to recommend her: and this approbation has become more general as the minds of men have grown more enlightned by that sound philosophy whose progress has been so rapid within these last forty years; a philosophy, which teaches us to pay only outward respect to greatness and authority, while we reserve our real respect and esteem for great abilities, when exerted for the public good.

I shall now relate with fidelity what I have met with touching this marriage in the dispatches of count Bassowitz, Aulic counseller at Vienna, and a long time minister from Holstein at the court of Russia; a person of great parts, and unblemished honesty, and whose memory is still held in the highest

highest esteem in Germany. In a letter of his he writes thus: "The Czarina had not only been an instrument in procuring Peter that reputation he was famed for, but also the main spring of preserving his life. This prince was subject to violent convulsion fits, which were thought to proceed from the effects of poison which had been given him when young. Catherine by her unwearied assiduity had found means to make the violence of his fits less felt, and the returns more seldom, by studying every thing that would please him, which made him sensible that he could not live without her, and therefore made her the partner of his throne and bed."

FORTUNE, which has furnished us with many extraordinary scenes in this part of the world, and had raised Catherine from the lowest abyss of misery and distress, to an exalted state of grandeur, brought about another extraordinary incident in her favour a few years after her marriage with the Czar, an account of which I find thus related in a curious manuscript of a person who was at that time in the Czar's service, and who speaks of it as a thing to which he was an eye witness.

AN envoy from King Augustus to the Czar, on his return to Dresden through Courland, putting up at an inn by the way, heard the voice of a person who seemed in great distress, and whom the people of the house were treating in an insulting manner: the stranger, with a proper tone of resentment, made answer, that they would not dare to use him thus, if he could but once come to the speech

of

of the Czar, at whose court he had perhaps greater friends than they imagined.

THE envoy, hearing this, had a curiosity to ask the man some questions, and from the answers he let fall, and a close examination of his face, he thought he saw in him some resemblance of the empress Catherine; and when he came to Dresden, he could not forbear writing to one of his friends at Petersburg concerning it. This letter, by accident, came to the Czar's hand, who immediately sent an order to prince Repnin, then governor of Riga, to endeavour to find out the person mentioned in the letter. Prince Repnin immediately dispatched a messenger to Mittau in Courland, who, on enquiry, found out the man, and learned that his name was Charles Scavronski; that he was the son of a Lithuanian gentleman, who had been killed in the Polish wars, and leaving two children in the cradle, a boy and a girl, who had neither of them received any other education than that which simple nature gives to those who are abandoned to the world, and destitute of every thing. Scavronski, who had been parted from his sister while they were both infants, knew nothing further of her than that she had been taken prisoner in Marienburg, in the year 1704, and supposed her to be still in the houshold of prince Menzikoff, where he imagined she might have bettered her condition.

PRINCE Repnin, agreeable to the particular orders he had received from the Czar, caused Scavronski to be seized, and brought to Riga, under pretence of some crime he was charged with; and to give a better colour to the matter, at his arrival there, a sham information was drawn up against him, and he was soon after sent from thence to Petersburg, under a strong guard, with orders that he should be well used upon the road.

When he arrived at Petersburg, he was carried to the house of an officer of the emperor's, named Shepleff, who having been instructed in the part he was to act, drew several circumstances from the young man in relation to his condition; and, after some time, told him, that although the information, which had been sent up from Riga against him, was of a very serious nature, yet he would have justice done him; but that it would be necessary to present a petition to his majesty for that purpose; that one should accordingly be drawn up in his name, and that he would find means that he should deliver it into the Czar's hands himself.

The next day the Czar came to dine with Shepleff at his own house, who presented Scavronski to him; when his majesty, after asking him abundance of questions, was convinced, by the artless answers he gave, of his being the real brother of the Czarina: they had both lived in Livonia when young, and the Czar found every thing that Scavronski said to him, in relation to his family-affairs, to tally exactly with what his spouse had told him concerning her brother, and the troubles which had befallen her and her brother in their childhood.

The Czar, now satisfied of the truth, proposed the next day to the empress to go and dine with him at Shepleff's; and when dinner was over, he ordered

ordered that the man whom he had examined the day before should be brought in again. Accordingly Scavronski was introduced, dressed in the same cloaths he had worn while on his journey from Riga, the Czar not being willing that he should appear in any other garb than what his poor circumstances had accustomed him to wear.

He examined him again in the presence of the Czarina, and the MS. adds, that he turned about to the empress, and said these very words, "This is your brother; come hither, Charles, and kiss the empress's hand, and embrace thy sister."

The author of this narrative adds further, that the empress fainted away with surprize; and that when she came to herself again, the Czar said to her, "There is nothing in this but what is very natural. This gentleman is my brother-in-law; if he has merit, we will make something of him; if he has not, we must leave him as he is."

This speech seems truly grand and noble. The author says, that Scavronski remained a considerable time at Shepleff's house; that a handsome pension was settled on him, but that he led a very retired life. Here he ends this relation, as his sole intention was only to disclose the secret of the empress's brother; but we know, from other authorities, that this gentleman was afterwards created a count; that he espoused a young lady of quality, by whom he had two daughters, who were married to two of the first noblemen in Russia. I leave to those who may be better informed of the particulars, to distinguish what is fact in this relation, from any

suppositious

suppositious additions, and shall only observe, that the author does not seem to have told this story with a design of only entertaining his readers with the marvellous, since his papers were not designed to be published. He writes freely to a friend concerning a thing of which he says he was an eyewitness. He may have been mistaken in some particulars, but the fact itself has all the appearance of truth; for if Charles had known that his sister was raised to so great a dignity, he would not certainly have delayed so many years without having made himself known to her. And this discovery, however extraordinary it may seem, is certainly not more so than the exaltation of Catherine herself: but the one and the other are a striking proof of the force of destiny, and may teach us to be cautious in treating things as fabulous, which perhaps are less contradictory to the common order of things, than the whole history of this empress.

THE entertainments which the Czar Peter gave, and the rejoicings that were made on the occasion, were not of that kind which exhaust the public treasury, for he carried on greater designs. He finished his grand foundery for cannon, and the admiralty buildings. He improved the roads, several ships were launched, and others put upon the stocks; canals were dug, a grand exchange and other buildings for the conveniency of commerce were built, and made the trade of Petersburg to flourish. He removed the senate from Moscow to Petersburg, in the month of April 1712. By this he made his new city the capital of the empire.

pire. He, at the same time, employed a number of Swedish prisoners in beautifying this city, whose foundation was owing to their defeat.

CHAP. IV.

Stetin taken.

Descent upon Finland. Events of the year 1712.

PETER, being happy in his family, and government, successful in his war against Charles XII. and in the several negociations with other powers, who were resolved to assist him in driving out the Swedes from the continent, and shutting them up for ever within the narrow peninsula of Scandinavia, began to turn his eyes entirely towards the western coasts of Europe, not laying aside all thoughts of the Palus Mæotis, or the Black Sea. The keys of Asoph were given up, and, notwithstanding all the intrigues of the king of Sweden, and of his friends at the Ottoman court, and even some surmises of a new war with the Turks, both Russia and Turky continued living in peace.

CHARLES XII. still obstinate, would continue at Bender, tamely submitting his hopes and fortunes to the caprice of a grand vizir; while the Czar was threatning all his provinces, had armed against him the king of Denmark, and the elector of Hanover, and had almost persuaded the king of Prussia, and even the Poles and Saxons, to declare openly against him.

CHARLES continuing still with the same inflexible pride, behaved in the like manner towards his enemies, who now seemed united to overwhelm him, as he had done before towards the Porte; and from his lonely prison, in the desarts of Bessarabia, braved the Czar, the kings of Poland, Denmark and Prussia, the elector of Hanover, soon afterwards king of England, and the emperor of Germany, whom he had so greatly offended, when he passed through Silesia as a conqueror, and now shewed his resentment, by abandoning him to his ill-fortune, and refused giving any protection to the territories which belonged to the Swedes in Germany.

IT would have been an easy matter for him to have broken the league which was forming against him, upon his yielding up Stetin in Pomerania *, to Frederic, the first king of Prussia, and elector of Brandenburg, who had a legal claim thereto: but Charles did not then look upon Prussia as a power of any consequence; and indeed neither he, nor any other person, could at that time foresee, that this small kingdom, and the electorate of Brandenburg, either of which were little better than desarts, would soon become formidable. Therefore he would not hearken to any proposal of accommodation, but determining rather to take all than

* 1712.

give up any thing, sent orders to the regency of Stockholm, to make all possible resistance both by sea and land; and these orders were obeyed, notwithstanding his dominions were almost drained of men and money. The senate of Stockholm fitted out a fleet of thirteen ships of the line, and every person capable of bearing arms became a soldier: in a word, the inflexible courage and pride of Charles seemed to animate all his subjects, who were almost as unfortunate as their king.

From Charles's conduct it can hardly be thought that he had fixed upon any regular plan. He had still a powerful party in Poland, which, with the assistance of the Crim Tartars, might have ravaged that wretched country, but were not able to replace king Stanislaus on the throne; and his hopes of engaging the Ottoman Porte to espouse his cause, or convincing the divan, that it was their interest to send ten or twelve thousand men to the assistance of his friends, under pretence, that the Czar still supported his ally Augustus in Poland, was absolutely chimerical.

He continued still at Bender,* to wait the event of these foolish projects, while the Russians, Danes, and Saxons, were over-running Pomerania. Peter took Catherine with him on this expedition. The king of Denmark had already made himself master of Stade, a sea port town in the duchy of Bremen; and the united forces of Russia, Saxony, and Denmark, were already before Stralsund.

* Sept. 1712.

King Staniſlaus †, now perceiving the deplorable ſtate of ſo many provinces, the impoſſibility of his recovering the crown of Poland, and every thing in confuſion by the inflexibility of Charles, called a meeting of the Swediſh generals, who were defending Pomerania with an army of eleven thouſand men, as the laſt reſource they had left in thoſe provinces.

He adviſed them to make their terms with king Auguſtus, offering himſelf to be the victim of this reconciliation. On this occaſion, he made the following ſpeech to them in the French language, which he afterwards left in writing, and which was ſigned by nine general officers. amongſt whom happened to be one Patkul, couſin-german to the unfortunate Patkul, whom Charles had cauſed to be broke on the wheel.

" Having been hitherto the inſtrument of pro-
" curing glory to the Swediſh arms, I will not now
" be the wretched cauſe of their ruin. I therefore
" declare that I ſacrifice the crown, and my own in-
" tereſts, to the preſervation of the ſacred perſon
" of the king, as I can ſee no other human means
" left of releaſing him from the place where he is
" at preſent."

Having made this declaration, he prepared to ſet out for Turky, in hopes of being able to ſoften the inflexible temper of his benefactor, by the ſacrifice he had made for him. His ill-fortune would have it, that he arrived in Beſſarabia, at the very

† October, 1712.

time that Charles, after having given his word to the sultan, that he would depart from Bender, and having received the neceſſary remittances for his journey, and an eſcort for his perſon, took the mad reſolution to continue there, and oppoſed a whole army of Turks and Tartars, with only his own domeſtics. The Turks, though they might eaſily have killed him, contented themſelves with taking him priſoner. At this very time, Staniſlaus arriving, was ſeized himſelf, ſo that two Chriſtian kings were priſoners at the ſame time in Turky.

At this time, when all Europe was in arms, and France had juſt terminated a war equally fatal againſt one part thereof, in order to ſettle the grandſon of Lewis XIV. on the throne of Spain, England gave peace to France, and the victory gained by Marſhal Villars at Denain in Flanders ſaved that nation from its other enemies. France had been for more than a century the ally of Sweden, and it was the intereſt of the former that its ally ſhould not loſe his poſſeſſions in Germany. Charles unhappily was at ſuch a diſtance from his dominions, that he did not even know what was doing in France.

The regency of Stockholm, by a deſperate effort, ventured to demand a ſum of money from the French court at a time when Lewis XIV had hardly money enough to pay his houſhold ſervants. Count Sparre was ſent with a commiſſion to negotiate this loan, in which he had no hopes of ſucceeding. However, on his arrival at Verſailles, he repreſented to the marquis de Torci the inability of the regency to pay the little army which

Charles

Charles had still remaining in Pomerania, and which was ready to break up on account of the long arrears due to the men; and that France was on the point of beholding the only ally she had left deprived of those territories which were so necessary to preserve the balance of power; that indeed his master Charles had not been altogether so attentive to the interests of France, as might have been expected, but that the magnanimity of Lewis XIV. was at least equal to the misfortunes of his royal brother and ally. The French minister, in answer to this speech, so effectually convinced the Swede of the incapacity of his court to furnish the requested succours, that count Sparre despaired of succeeding.

WHAT Sparre had despaired of was done by a private citizen. There was at that time in Paris a banker named Samuel Bernard, who had a large fortune by making remittances for the government to foreign countries, and other private contracts. This man was intoxicated with a species of honour very rarely to be met with amongst people of his profession. He was immoderately fond of every thing that made him talked of, and knew very well that one time or another the government would repay with interest those who hazarded their fortune to supply its exigencies. Count Sparre dining one day with this man, took care to flatter his foible so well, that before rising from the table the banker put six hundred thousand livres into his hand; and then immediately waiting on the marquis de Torci, he said to him, "I have lent the crown of Sweden

six

six hundred thousand livres in your name, which you must repay me when you are able"

Count Steinbock, general of Charles's army, little expected such a supply; and observing his troops so ready to mutiny, to whom he had nothing to give but promises, and that the storm was gathering fast upon him, and being moreover apprehensive of being surrounded by the three different armies of Russia, Denmark, and Saxony, had desired a cessation of arms, on the supposition that Stanislaus's abdication and his presence would remove the obstinacy of Charles, and that the only way left him to save the forces under his command, was by spinning out the time in negotiations. He therefore dispatched a courier to Bender, to represent to the king of Sweden the desperate state of his finances and affairs, and the situation of his army, and to acquaint him that he had, under these circumstances, found himself under a necessity to apply for a cessation of arms, which he should reckon himself happy to obtain. The courier had not been dispatched above three days, and Stanislaus was not yet set out on his journey to Bender, when Steinbock received the six hundred thousand livres from the French banker; a sum which was at that time an immense treasure in a country so desolated. Thus unexpectedly reinforced with money, which is the grand *panacea* for all disorders of state, Steinbock found means to revive the drooping spirits of his soldiery; he supplied them with all they wanted, raised new recruits, and in a short time saw himself at the head of twelve thousand men, and dropping

ping his former intention of procuring a suspension of arms, he sought only for an opportunity of engaging the enemy.

This was the same Steinbock, who, in the year 1710, after the defeat at Pultowa, had revenged the Swedes on the Danes by the eruption he made into Scania, where he marched against and engaged them with only a few militia, whom he had gathered together in a hurry, with their arms slung round them with ropes, and totally defeated the enemy. He was like all the other generals of Charles XII. active and enterprising; but his valour was sullied by his brutality: as an instance of which it will be sufficient to relate, that having, after an engagement with the Russians, given orders to kill all the prisoners, and perceiving a Polish officer in the service of the Czar who had caught hold of king Stanislaus's stirrup, then on horseback, in order to save his life, Steinbock shot him dead with his pistol in that prince's arms, as has been already mentioned in the life of Charles XII and king Stanislaus has declared to the author of this history, that had he not been with-held by his respect and gratitude to the king of Sweden, he should immediately have shot Steinbock dead upon the spot.

General Steinbock now marched, by the way of Wismaar to meet the combined forces of the Russians, Danes, and Saxons ‡, and soon found himself near the Danish and Saxon army, which was advanced before that of the Russians about the

‡ Decr. 9. 1712.

distance

distance of three leagues. The Czar sent three couriers, one after another, to the king of Denmark, beseeching him to wait his coming up, and thereby avoid the danger which threatened him if he attempted to engage the Swedes with an inequality of force; but the Danish monarch not willing to share with any one the honour of a victory which he thought sure, advanced to meet the Swedish-general, whom he attacked near the place called Gadebusch. This day's action was a fresh proof of the natural enmity that subsisted between the Swedes and Danes. The officers of these two nations rushing furiously on one another, fought with great bravery, till death parted them.

STEINBOCK gained a compleat victory before the Russian army could come to the assistance of the Danes, and the next day received an order from his master Charles to lay aside all thoughts of a suspension of arms, who at the same time upbraided him for having entertained a thought so injurious to his honour, and for which he told him he could make no reparation, but by conquering or perishing. Steinbock had happily obtained a victory, so that there was no occasion for obeying these orders.

But this victory was like that which had formerly brought such a transient consolation to king Augustus, when in the torrent of his misfortunes he gained the battle of Calish against the Swedes, who were conquerors in every other place, and which only served to aggravate his situation, as this of Gadebusch only retarded the ruin of Steinbock and his army.

WHEN

WHEN the king of Sweden received advice of Steinbock's succefs, he imagined his affairs once more on a good footing, and flattered himfelf with hopes to engage the Ottoman Porte to declare for him, who at that time feemed inclined to come to a new rupture with the Czar. Full of thefe fond imaginations, he fent orders to general Steinbock to fall upon Poland, being ftill ready to believe, upon the leaft fuccefs, that the days of Narva, and thofe in which he gave laws to his enemies, were again returned. But unhappily he too foon found thefe flattering hopes utterly blafted by the affair of Bender, and his own captivity in Turky.

THE whole fruits of the victory at Gadebufch were confined to the furprifing in the night time, and reducing to afhes the town Altena, inhabited by traders and manufacturers, a place wholly defencelefs, and which not having been in arms, ought by all the laws of war and nations to have been fpared: however, it was utterly deftroyed; feveral of the inhabitants perifhed in the flames, others efcaped with their lives, but naked; and a number of old men, women, and children, died with cold and the fatigue they fuffered, at the gates of Hamburgh ‡. Such has too often been the fate of feveral thoufands of men for the quarrels of two only; and this cruel advantage was the only one gained by Steinbock; for the Ruffians, Danes, and Saxons, purfued him fo clofely, that he was oblig-

‡ Norberg the king's chaplain and confeffor, in his hiftory, coolly fays, that general Steinbock fet fire to the town, only becaufe he had not carriages to bring away the furniture.

ed to beg shelter for himself and his army in Toningen, a fortress in the duchy of Holstein.

HOLSTEIN was at that time a most desolate country, and its sovereign was in the most miserable condition. He was nephew to Charles XII. and it was on his father's account, who had married Charles's sister, that that monarch carried his arms even into the heart of Copenhagen, before the battle of Narva, and for whom he likewise made the treaty of Travendahl, by which the dukes of Holstein recovered their rights.

THIS country was part of the nursery of the Cimbri, and of the old Normans, who over-run the province of Neustria in France, and conquered all England, Naples, and Sicily; and yet at present no state is less able to make conquests than this part of the ancient Cimbrica Chersonesus, which consists only of two small duchies; namely, that of Slefwick, belonging in common to the king of Denmark and the duke of Holstein, and that of Gottorp, to the duke alone. Slefwick is a sovereign principality: Holstein is a branch of the German empire, called the Roman empire.

THE king of Denmark and the duke of Holstein Gottorp were of the same house; but the duke, nephew to Charles XII. and presumptive heir to his crown, was the natural enemy of the king of Denmark, who had always wanted to crush him, even from his infancy. The bishop of Lubeck, administrator of the dominions of this unfortunate prince, now beheld himself in the midst of the Swedish army, whom he durst not succour, and those of
Russia,

Russia, Denmark, and Saxony, that threatened his country with daily destruction. Nevertheless he thought himself obliged to try to save Charles's army, if he could do it without irritating the king of Denmark, who had made himself master of his country, depopulating and draining it of all its substance.

This bishop and administrator of Holstein was entirely governed by the famous baron Goertz, the most crafty and enterprising man of his age, who had a genius amazingly penetrating, and fruitful in every resource: with talents equal to the boldest and most arduous attempts, he was as insinuating in his negotiations, as he was daring in his schemes. He had the art of pleasing and persuading in the highest degree, and knew how to captivate all hearts by the vivacity of his genius, after he had won them by the softness of his eloquence. He afterwards gained the same ascendant over Charles XII. which he had then over the bishop; and every one knows, that his head paid for the honour he had of governing the most ungovernable and obstinate prince that ever filled the throne.

Goertz had a private conference with general Steinbock ‡, and promised to deliver up the fortress of Toningen, without exposing the bishop administrator his master to any danger, and at the same time promised the king of Denmark, that he would defend the place to the last. In this manner are almost all negotiations carried on, affairs of state

‡ Private memoirs of Bassowitz, Jan. 21. 1712.

being

being of a very different nature from those of private persons; the honour of ministers consisting wholly in success, and those of private persons in the observance of their promises.

GENERAL Steinbock presented himself before Toningen; the commandant refused to open the gates to him, and by this means put it out of the king of Denmark's power to alledge any cause of complaint against the bishop administrator; but Goertz caused an order to be given in the name of the young duke, a minor, for permitting the Swedish army to enter the town. The secretary of the cabinet, named Stamke, signs this order in the name of the duke of Holstein: by this means Goertz preserves the honour of an infant who had not as yet any power to issue orders; and he at once serves the king of Sweden, to whom he was desirous to make his court, and the bishop administrator his master, who appeared not to have consented to the admission of the Swedish troops. The governor of Toningen, who was easily gained, delivered up the town to the Swedes, and Goertz excused himself as well as he could to the king of Denmark, by protesting that the whole had been transacted contrary to his advice.

THE Swedes retired partly within the walls, and partly under the cannon of the town*: but this did not save them; for general Steinbock was obliged to surrender himself prisoner of war, together with his whole army, to the number of eleven thousand

* Bassowitz's memoirs.

men,

men, in the fame manner as about fixteen thoufand of their countrymen had done at the battle of Pultowa.

It was agreed by this convention, that Steinbock, with his officers and men, might be ranfomed or exchanged. The price for the general's ranfom was fixed at eight thoufand imperial crowns; a very trifling fum, but which Steinbock however was not able to raife; fo that he remained a prifoner in Copenhagen till his death

The territories of Holftein now remained at the mercy of the incenfed conqueror. The young duke became the object of the king of Denmark's vengeance, and was obliged to pay for the abufe which Goertz had made of his name: thus did the ill fortune of Charles XII. fall upon all his family.

Goertz, though his projects were baffled, being ftill refolved to act a diftinguifhed part in this general confufion, recalled to mind a fcheme which he had formed to eftablifh a neutrality in the Swedifh territories in Germany.

The king of Denmark was at the gates of Toningen; George, elector of Hanover, was about to feize Bremen and Verden, with the city of Stade; the new-made king of Pruffia, Frederic William, caft his views upon Stetin, and Czar Peter was preparing to make himfelf mafter of Finland; and all the territories of Charles XII. thofe of Sweden excepted, were going to become the fpoils of thofe who wanted to fhare them. How then could fo many different interefts be reconciled with a neutrality?

trality? Goertz entered into negotiation at the same time with all the several princes concerned in this partition; he continued night and day going from one province to the other; he engaged the governor of Bremen and Verden to put those two duchies into the hands of the elector of Hanover by way of sequestration, so that the Danes should not seize them for themselves: he prevailed with the king of Prussia to accept jointly with the duke of Holstein, of the sequestration of Stetin and Wismaar, in consideration of which the king of Denmark was to act nothing against Holstein, and was not to enter Toningen. It was most certainly a strange way of serving Charles XII. to put his towns into the hands of those who might chuse if they would ever restore them; but Goertz, by delivering these places to them as pledges, bound them to a neutrality, at least for some time; and he was in hopes to be able afterwards to bring Hanover and Brandenburg to declare for Sweden; he prevailed on the king of Prussia, whose ruined dominions stood in need of peace, to enter into his views; and in short, he found means to render himself necessary to all these princes, and disposed of the possessions of Charles XII. like a guardian, who gives up one of his ward's estates to preserve the other, and of a ward incapable of managing his affairs himself; and all this without any regular authority or commission, or any other warrant for his conduct, than full powers given him by the bishop of Lubeck, who had no authority to grant such powers from Charles himself.

THIS

THIS was Goertz's character, though not hitherto sufficiently known. There have been instances of an Oxenstiern, a Richlieu, and an Alberoni, influencing the affairs of all parts of Europe; but that the privy counsellor of a bishop of Lubeck should do the same as they, without being owned by any king, is something extraordinary.

NEVERTHELESS, in the beginning *, he succeeded better than he could have expected; for he made a treaty with the king of Prussia, by which that monarch engaged, on condition of keeping Stetin in sequestration, to preserve the rest of Pomerania for Charles XII. In consequence of this treaty Goertz made a proposal to the governor of Pomerania, Mayerfield, to give up the fortress of Stetin to the king of Prussia for the sake of peace, thinking that the Swedish governor of Stetin would prove as easy to be persuaded as the Holsteiner who had the command of Loningen; but the officers of Charles XII were not accustomed to obey such orders. Mayerfield made answer, that if Stetin was entered, it should be over his dead body and the ruins of the place, and immediately gave notice to his master of the strange proposal. The messenger at his arrival found Charles prisoner at Demirtash, in consequence of his adventure at Bender, and it was doubtful at that time, whether he would not remain all his life confined in Turky, or else be banished to some of the islands in the Archipelago, or some part of Asia under the dominion of the Otto-

* June 1713.

man

man Porte. However, Charles sent the same orders to Mayerfield, as he had done before to Steinbock; namely, rather to perish than submit to his enemies, and even commanded him to be as inflexible as himself.

GOERTZ finding that the governor of Stetin had broke in upon his measures, and would neither hearken to a neutrality nor a sequestration, formed a project not only to sequester the town of Stetin, but also the city of Stralsund, and found means to make the same kind of treaty with the king of Poland †, elector of Saxony, for that place, which he had done with the elector of Brandenburg for Stetin. He clearly saw how impossible it would be for the Swedes to keep possession of those places without either men or money, while their king was a captive in Turky, and he thought himself sure of turning aside the scourge of war from the north by means of these sequestrations. The king of Denmark himself at length gave into the projects of Goertz: the latter had gained an entire ascendant over prince Menzikoff, the Czar's general and favourite, whom he had persuaded that the duchy of Holstein must be ceded to his master, and flattered the Czar with the project of opening a canal from Holstein into the Baltic Sea; an enterprize perfectly conformable to the inclination and views of this royal founder; and above all, he laboured to insinuate to him that he might obtain a new increase of power, by condescending to be-

† June 1713.

come one of the princes of the empire, which would
entitle him to a vote at the diet of Ratifbon, a
right that he might afterwards maintain by a good
army.

IN fine, no perfon could put on more different
appearances, adapt himfelf to more oppofite inte-
rells, or act a more complicated part, than did this
fkilful negotiator He even went fo far as to engage prince Menzikoff to deftroy the town of Stetin, which he was endeavouring to fave, by bom-
barding it, in order to force Mayerfield to feque-
fter it into his hands, and offered this unpardona-
ble infult to the king of Sweden, into whofe favour he endeavoured to ingratiate himfelf; and in
which, at length, to his lofs, he fucceeded but too
well.

WHEN the king of Pruffia faw a Ruffian army
before Stetin, he found that place would be loft to
him, and would fall into the hands of the Czar.
This was juft what Goertz expected and waited
for. Prince Menzikoff was in want of money;
Goertz got the king of Pruffia to lend him four
hundred thoufand crowns; he afterwards fent a mef-
fenger to the governor of the place, to know of him,
" whether he would rather chufe to fee Stetin in
afhes, and under the dominion of Ruffia, or truft
it in the hands of the king of Pruffia, who would
engage to reftore it to the king his mafter?" The
commandant at length complied, and gave up the
place, which Menzikoff entered; and in confidera-
tion of the four hundred thoufand crowns delivered
it afterwards, together with the territories thereto
adjoining,

adjoining, in the hands of the king of Prussia, who, for form's sake, left therein two battalions of the troops of Holstein, but has never since restored that part of Pomerania.

The baron de Goertz, who put so many springs in motion, could not however succeed in prevailing on the Danes to spare the duchy of Holstein, or forbear taking possession of Toningen. He failed in what appeared to have been his first object, though he succeeded in all his other views, and particularly in that of making himself a person of the most importance in the north, which indeed was his chief design.

The elector of Hanover had already secured to himself Bremen and Verden, of which Charles XII. was now stripped. The Saxon army was now before Wismaar; Stetin was in the hands of the king of Prussia †: the Russians were ready to lay siege to Stralsund, in conjunction with the Saxons; and these latter had already landed in the island of Rugen; and the Czar, in the midst of the numberless negotiations on all sides, while others were disputing about neutralities and partitions, made a descent in Finland. After having himself pointed the artillery against Stralsund, he left the rest to the care of his allies and prince Menzikoff, and embarked in the month of May, on the Baltic Sea, on board a ship of fifty guns, built from a model of his own making at Petersburg; he sailed for the coast of Finland, followed by a fleet of ninety-two

† Sept. 1715.

whole, and one hundred and ten half galleys, having on board near sixteen thousand land forces §. He made a defcent at Helfinfort, the moft fouthern part of that cold and barren country, lying in fixty-one degrees north latitude; and notwthftanding the numberlefs difficulties he had to encounter, fucceeded in his defign. He made a faint attack on one fide of the harbour, while he landed his troops on the other, and took poffeffion of the town. He then made himfelf mafter of Abo, Borgo, and the whole coaft. The Swedes now feemed not to have any refource left; for it was, at this very time, that their army, under the command of general Steinbock, had furrendered prifoners of war.

ALL thefe loffes and diftreffes were followed by the lofs of Bremen, Verden, Stetin, and a part of Pomerania; and Charles himfelf, with his ally and friend Stanifaus, were both prifoners in Turky: neverthelefs, he flattered himfelf with the hopes of returning to Poland, at the head of an army of Turks, replacing Stanifaus on the throne, and once again making all his enemies tremble.

§ May 22. 1713. N. S.

CHAP.

CHAP. V.

Successes of Peter the Great.

Charles XII. returns into his dominions.

PETER, notwithstanding his conquests†, was compleating his naval establishment, brought twelve thousand families to settle in Petersburg, kept all his allies steady to his person and fortunes, though they had all different interests, and many of their views quite opposite; and with his fleet, kept in awe all the sea-ports of Sweden on the gulphs of Finland and Bothnia.

PRINCE Galitzin, one of his land-generals, whom he had trained up himself, as he had done all his other officers, advanced from Helsinfort, where the Czar had made his descent, into the midst of the country, near the village of Tavasthus, which was a post that commanded the gulph of Bothnia, and defended by a few Swedish regiments, and about eight thousand militia. In this situation a battle ensued ‡, the event of which proved favourable to the Russians, who entirely routed the whole Swedish army, and penetrated as far as Vaza, so that they were now in possession of about fourscore leagues of country.

† 1713, 1714.   ‡ March 12, 1714.

The Swedes were still in possession of a fleet, with which they kept the sea. Peter greatly wished for an opportunity of signalizing his naval force, which he had entirely planned himself. Accordingly he set out from Petersburg, and having got together a fleet of sixteen ships of the line, and one hundred and eighty galleys, fit for working among the rocks and shoals that surround the island of Aland, and the other islands in the Baltic Sea, bordering upon the Swedish coast, he fell in with the fleet o that nation near their own shores. This armament greatly exceeded his in the largeness of the ships, but was inferior in the number of galleys, and more proper for engaging in the open sea, than among rocks, or near the shore. The advantage the Czar had in this respect, was entirely owing to his own genius. He served in the rank of rear admiral on board his own fleet, and received all the necessary orders from admiral Apraxin. Peter resolved to make himself master of the island of Aland, which lies only twelve leagues from Sweden; to accomplish this, he was obliged to pass full in view of the enemy's fleet. His galleys forced a passage through the enemy, whose cannon did not fire low enough to hurt them, and entered Aland; but as that coast is almost surrounded with rocks, the Czar caused eighty small galleys to be carried by men, over a point of land, and launched into the sea, at a place called Hango, where his large ships were at anchor Erenschild, the Swedish rear admiral, who thought he would have no difficulty in taking or sinking these galleys, stood

on

on shore, in order to reconnoitre their situation; but was received with so brisk a fire from the Russian fleet, that most of his men were killed or wounded; and the galleys and prames he had brought with him were taken, together with the ship on board of which he had hoisted his flag He himself endeavoured to escape in a boat*; but being wounded, was obliged to surrender himself prisoner, and was brought on board the galley which was worked by the Czar. The scattered remains of the Swedish fleet made the best of their way home. This news alarmed all Sweden, and even Stockholm did not think itself safe.

Much about the same time, colonel Schouvalow Neushlot attacked the only remaining fortress on the western side of Finland, and made himself master of it, after a most obstinate resistance.

The sea-fight of Aland was, next to that of the battle of Pultowa, the most glorious that had ever happened to Peter the Great, who was now master of Finland, the government of which he committed to prince Galitzin, and returned to Petersburg †; triumphing over the whole naval force of Sweden, and respected by his allies more than ever: the tempestuous season coming on, did not permit him to remain longer with his ships in the Finlandish and Bothnic seas. And to crown his joy, upon his arrival at Petersburg, the Czarina was brought to bed of a princess, who died, however, about a year afterwards. He then instituted the order of St.

* Aug. 8. † Sept. 15.

D 4 Catherine,

Catherine, in honour of his confort, and celebrated the birth of his daughter by a triumphal entry, which was, of all the feftivals to which he had accuftomed his people, that which they were fondeft of. This ceremony was begun by bringing nine Swedifh galleys, and feven prames filled with prifoners, and rear-admiral Erenfchild's own fhip, into the harbour of Conftadt.

THE cannon, colours, and ftandards taken in the expedition to Finland, which the Ruffian admiral's fhip had on board, were brought on this occafion to Peterfburg, and entered that metropolis in order of battle. A triumphal arch which the Czar had caufed to be erected, and which, as ufual, was made from a model of his own defigning, was decorated with the emblems of his conquefts. Under this arch the victors marched in proceffion, headed by admiral Apraxin; then the Czar followed, in quality of rear-admiral, and the other officers according to their feveral ranks. They were prefented one after another to vice admiral Romadonofki, who, at this ceremony, reprefented the fovereign of the empire. This temporary vice-emperor diftributed gold medals among the officers, and the foldiers and failors had filver ones. The Swedifh prifoners alfo paffed under the triumphal arch, and admiral Erenfchild followed immediately after the Czar, his conqueror. When they came to the place where the vice Czar was feated on his throne, admiral Apraxin prefented to him rear-admiral Peter, who demanded to be made vice admiral, in regard for his fervices. It was then put

to

to the vote, if this requeſt ſhould be granted; and it may eaſily be thought that he had the majority for him.

After this ceremony was over, which filled every heart with joy, and inſpired every mind with emulation, with a love for his country, and a thirſt of fame, the Czar made the following ſpeech to thoſe preſent; a ſpeech which deſerves to be tranſmitted to the lateſt poſterity.

"Countrymen and friends, is there any man among you, who could have thought, twenty years ago, that we ſhould one day fight together on the Baltic Sea, in ſhips built by our own hands; and that we ſhould eſtabliſh ſettlements in countries conquered by our own courage and valour?——— Greece is ſaid to have been the ancient ſeat of the arts and ſciences; they afterwards took up their abode in Italy, from whence they ſpread themſelves through every part of Europe. It is now our turn to call them ours, if you will ſecond my deſigns, by adding obedience to ſtudy. The arts circulate in this world, as the blood does in the human body; and I make no doubt they will eſtabliſh their empire amongſt us, on their return back to Greece, their native country; and I even venture to affirm, that our noble labours will terminate in ſo ſolid a glory, that it will make the moſt civilized nations bluſh."

This is the ſubſtance of this ſpeech, ſo worthy of a great founder, the chief beauties of which have been loſt in this, as well as every other tranſlation; but the principal merit of this eloquent harangue is its having been spoken by a victorious monarch, at once the founder and law-giver of his empire.

The old boyars heard this harangue with greater regret for the abolition of their ancient customs, than joy for their master's glory; but the young ones with tears of joy received it.

The joy of the Russians was further heightened by the return of the Russian ambassador from Constantinople, with a confirmation of the peace with the Turks†: and an ambassador a little before had arrived from Sha Hussein of Persia, with a present to the Czar of an elephant and five lions. He received at the same time an ambassador from Mehemet Bahadir, khan of the Usbeck Tartars, requesting his protection against another tribe of Tartars; so that both extremities of Asia and Europe seemed to join to pay their homage to him, and to advance his glory.

The regency of Stockholm, become desperate by the situation of their affairs, and the absence of their sovereign, who seemed to have abandoned his dominions, had come to a resolution no more to consult him in relation to their proceedings; and immediately after the victory the Czar gained over their navy, they sent to the conqueror to demand a passport for an officer charged with proposals of peace. This passport was sent; but just as the person appointed to carry on the negotiation was on the point of setting out, the princess Ulrica Eleo-

† Sept. 15. 1714.

nora,

norar fifter to Charles XII. received advice from the king her brother, that he was at length preparing to quit Turky, and return home to fight his own battles. This put a stop to the negotiator's journey (whom they had already privately named) to the Czar: and they came to a resolution of nobly supporting their losses till Charles should come to retrieve them.

CHARLES, after a stay of five years and some months in Turky, set out from that kingdom in the latter end of October 1714. It is known that he observed the same singularity in his journey, which characterized all his actions. He arrived at Stralsund the twenty-second of November following. As soon as he got there, baron de Goertz came to pay his court to him; and though he had been the author of one part of his misfortunes, yet he justified his conduct with so much art, and filled the imagination of Charles with such brilliant hopes, that he gained his confidence, as he had already done that of every other minister and prince with whom he had entered into any negotiations. In fine, he made him believe, that he could detatch the Czar's allies, and thereby procure an honourable peace, or at least to carry on the war upon an equal footing; add from this time Goertz obtained a greater sway over the mind of king Charles than ever count Piper had.

THE first thing Charles did after his arrival at Stralsund, was to demand a supply of money from the citizens of Stockholm, who readily parted with what little they had left, as not being able to refuse any thing to a king, who asked only to bestow, who lived as hard as the meanest soldier, and exposed his life equally in defence of his country. His misfortunes, his captivity, his return to his dominions, so long deprived of his presence, were arguments which prepossessed alike his own subjects and foreigners in his favour, who could not forbear at once to blame and admire, to compassionate and to assist him. The glory he pursued differed widely from that of Peter the Great; it consisted not in cherishing the arts and sciences, in enacting laws, in establishing a form of government, nor in introducing commerce among his subjects; it was confined entirely to his own person. He placed his chief merit in a valour superior to what is commonly called courage. He defended his dominions with a greatness of soul equal to his valour, his chief design being to inspire other nations with awe and respect for him; hence he had more well-wishers than allies.

CHAP. VI.

State of Europe at the return of Charles XII.
Siege of Stralfund.

CHARLES XII. when he came back to his kingdom in the year 1714, found the state of affairs in Christian Europe in a quite different state from that in which he had left them. Queen Anne of England was dead, after having made peace with France. Lewis XIV. had secured Spain, and had obliged the emperor Charles VI. and the Hollanders to sign a necessary peace ; so that all the affairs of Europe had quite a different face.

Those of the north had undergone a still greater change. Peter was now become arbiter in that part of the world: the elector of Hanover, who had been called to fill the British throne, had views of extending his territories in Germany, at the expence of Sweden, who had never had any possessions in that country, but since the reign of the great Gustavus. The king of Denmark aimed at recovering Scania, the best province in Sweden, which had formerly belonged to the Danes. The king of Prussia, heir to the duke of Pomerania, laid claim to a part of that province. On the other hand, the house of Holstein, oppressed by the king of Denmark, and the duke of Mecklenburg,

almost

almoſt at open war with his ſubjects, were begging Peter the Great to take them under his protection. The king of Poland, elector of Saxony, was deſirous to have the duchy of Courland annexed to Poland; thus from the Elbe to the Baltic Sea, as Charles had been the terror of the ſeveral crowned heads, ſo Peter was now become their ſupport.

MANY negotiations were ſet on foot after the return of Charles to his dominions, but nothing could be done. Charles thought he could raiſe a ſufficient number of ſhips of war and privateers, to cruſh the riſing power of the Czar by ſea; with reſpect to the land-war, he relied upon his own courage; and Goertz, who was on a ſudden become his prime miniſter, perſuaded him, that he might find means to defray the expence, by coining copper money, to be taken at ninety ſix times more than its real value, a never heard of prodigy in the hiſtories of any ſtate; but, as early as the month of April 1715 the firſt Swediſh privateers that put to ſea were taken by the Czar's men of war, and a Ruſſian army advanced into Pomerania.

THE Pruſſians, Danes, and Saxons, joined their forces in attacking Stralſund; and Charles XII. ſaw himſelf returned from his confinement at Demirtaſh and Demirtoca on the Black ſea, only to be more cloſely confined on the borders of the Baltic Sea.

WE have already ſeen with what bold and tranquil valour he defied the united forces of all his enemies

nemies when in Stralfund; and fhall therefore, in this place, only add a fingle circumflance, that may ferve to fhew his character. The greateft part of his officers having been either killed or wounded during this fiege, the duty fell hard upon the few who were left. Baron de Reichel, a colonel, having fuftained a long engagement upon the ramparts, and being tired out with repeated watches, old age, and fatigues, had thrown himfelf upon a bench to take an hour's fleep. When he was called up to mount guard again upon the ramparts, as he was dragging himfelf along, hardly able to ftand, and curfing the obftinacy of the king his mafter, who fubjected all thofe about him to fuch infufferable and fruitlefs fatigues, Charles happened to overhear him: upon which, ftripping off his own cloak, he fpread it on the ground before him, faying, "My dear Reichel, you are quite fpent, come, I have had an hour's fleep, which has refrefhed me, I'll take the guard for you, while you finifh your nap, and will wake you when it is time;" and faying this, he wrapt the colonel up in his cloak; and notwithftanding all his refiftance, obliged him to lie down to fleep, and mounted the guard for him.

It was during this famous fiege that the elector of Hanover, the new king of England, purchafed of the king of Denmark the province of Bremen and Verden, with the city of Stade *, which the Danes had taken from Charles XII. This purchafe

* Oct. 1715.

cost king George eight hundred thousand German crowns. In this manner were the dominions of Charles bartered away, while he defended the city of Stralsund, inch by inch, till at length nothing was left of it but a heap of ruins, which his officers compelled him to leave †; and when he was in a place of safety, general Duker delivered up those ruins to the king of Prussia.

Some time afterwards, Duker being presented to Charles, that monarch reproached him with having capitulated with his enemies; when Duker replied, "I had your glory too much at heart, to continue to defend a place which you was obliged to leave." However, the Prussians continued in possession of it no longer than the year 1721, when it was given up at the general peace.

During the siege of Stralsund, Charles received another mortification, which would have given him great pain, if his heart had been as sensible of friendship, as it was of military glory. His prime minister count Piper, a man well known throughout all Europe, and of unshaken fidelity to his prince (notwithstanding the false assertions of an indiscreet writer :) Piper, I say, had been the victim of his master's ambition ever since the battle of Pultowa. No cartel being at that time settled for the exchange of prisoners between the Russians and Swedes, he had remained in confinement at Moscow; and although he had not been sent into Siberia, as the other prisoners were, his situation was

† Dec. 13.

still

still to be pitied. The Czar's finances at that time were not managed with such fidelity as they ought to have been, and his many new establishments required an expence which it was difficult for him to answer. He owed a considerable sum of money to the Dutch, on account of two of their merchantships which had been burned on the coast of Finland, in the descent the Czar had made on that country. Peter pretended that the Swedes were to pay the money, and wanted count Piper to charge himself with that debt: accordingly he was sent for from Moscow to Petersburg, and his liberty was offered him, in case he could draw bills of exchange upon Sweden for sixty thousand crowns. It is said that he actually did draw bills for this sum upon his lady at Stockholm, but that she being either unable or unwilling to answer them, they were returned, and the king of Sweden never gave himself the least concern about paying the money. Be this as it will, count Piper was closely confined in the castle of Schluffelburg, where he died the year after, at seventy years of age. His remains were sent to the king of Sweden, who gave them a magnificent burial; a melancholy recompence for a life of such faithful services, and so miserable an end!

PETER was satisfied with having got possession of Livonia, Estonia, Carelia, and Ingria, which he looked upon as provinces belonging to his dominions, and to which he had, moreover, added almost all Finland, which served as a kind of security, in case his enemies should conclude a peace. He had
married

married one of his nieces to Charles Leopold, duke of Mecklenburg *, so that all the sovereigns of the north were now either his allies or his creatures. In Poland, he kept the enemies of king Augustus in awe; one of his armies, consisting of about eight thousand men, having, without any loss, quelled several of those rebellions, which are so frequent in that country of liberty and anarchy: on the other hand, the Turks, faithfully observing their treaties, he had full power and time to execute all his projects.

In this peaceful flourishing state of affairs, not a day passed without producing some new establishments, either in the army, or the navy, with respect to commerce, or the laws; he himself drew up a military code for the infantry.

He likewise founded a naval academy at Petersburg †; sent Lange to China by the way of Siberia, with a commission of trade: employed mathematicians in drawing charts of the whole empire; built a fine summer palace at Petershoff; built forts on the banks of the Irtish, stopped the incursions and ravages of the Bukari on the one side, and, on the other, suppressed the Kouban Tartars.

His prosperity seemed now to be at its zenith ‡; he seemed now to have arrived at the top of his prosperity, and still to add to his felicity, the empress Catherine was delivered of a son, and an heir to his dominions, by a prince being born to his son the Czarowitz Alexis. But this joy was soon damped

* 1715.   † Nov. 8.   ‡ 1715.

by

by the death of the empress's son; and the sequel of this history will shew us the tragical end of Alexis, so that the birth of a son to him could not be reckoned a real happiness.

The delivery of the Czarina put a hindrance to her attending him, as usual, in all his expeditions by sea and land; but as soon as she was recovered she accompanied him to new adventures.

CHAP. VII.

Wismar taken. New travels of the Czar.

WISMAR was now besieged by all the Czar's allies. This town, which belonged of right to the duke of Mecklenburg, is situated on the Baltic, above seven leagues distant from Lubeck, and might have rivalled that city in its extensive trade, being once one of the most considerable of the Hanse Towns. The duke of Mecklenburg was rather a protector than a sovereign of it. This was one of the German territories which the Swedes possessed, in virtue of the peace of Westphalia: but it was now obliged to surrender. The allies of the Czar pushed the siege with the greatest vigour, in order to be masters of it before his troops arrived: but Peter himself coming before the place in person, after the capitulation †,

† Feb. 1716.

which had been made without consulting him, made the garrison prisoners of war. He was not a little provoked, that his allies should have left the king of Denmark in possession of a town which was the right of a prince who had married his neice; and his resentment on this occasion, which that artful minister de Goertz soon after turned to his own advantage, laid the first foundation of the peace, which he meditated to bring about between Charles XII. and the Czar.

GOERTZ now represented to the Czar, that Sweden was sufficiently weakened, and that he should be cautious to let Denmark and Prussia become too powerful. The Czar was of the same opinion with him, and as he had entered into the war merely from motives of policy, he, from that instant, did not push his operations against Sweden; and Charles, every where unfortunate in Germany, determined to risk one of those desperate strokes, which success only can justify, and carried the war into Norway.

PETER thought he had now time to make a second tour through Europe. He undertook his first, as one who wanted instruction in the arts and sciences; but his second, as a prince, who wanted to come at the secrets of foreign courts. He carried the Czarina with him to Copenhagen, Lubeck, Schwerin, and Nystadt. He had an interview with the king of Prussia at the little town of Aversberg, from thence he and the empress went to Hamburg, and to Altena, which had lately been burned by the Swedes, and which they were now rebuilding.

rebuilding. Descending the Elbe as far as Stade, they passed through Bremen, where the magistrates entertained them with fire-works and illuminations, which formed, in different places, these words, "Our deliverer is come amongst us §." At length he came to Amsterdam, and visited his little hut at Saardam, where he had formerly learned the art of ship-building, and found his old dwelling converted into a magnificent house, which is still to be seen, and goes by the name of the prince's house.

It may easily be conceived, with what joy and adulation he was received by a trading and sea-faring people, whose companion he had been, and they looked on the conqueror of Pultowa as a scholar who had learned from them to gain naval victories; and to follow their example, in establishing trade and navigation in his own empire. In fine, they looked upon him as one of their fellow-citizens, who had been raised to the imperial dignity.

A surprising difference may be observed in the life, the travels, the actions of Peter the Great, and of Charles of Sweden, to the manners which prevail among us, and which are rather too effeminate; and this is one reason, that the history of these two famous men so much excite our curiosity.

The Czarina had stayed at Schwerin indisposed, being far advanced in her pregnancy; but, as

§ Dec. 17. 1716.

soon as she was able to travel, she proceeded to join the Czar in Holland, but was taken in labour at Wesel, and there delivered of a prince †, who died next day. It is not customary amongst us for a lying-in-woman to go abroad for some time; but the Czarina set out, and arrived at Amsterdam in ten days after her labour. She was very desirous to see the little hut her husband had lived and worked in. Accordingly she and the Czar went together, attended by two servants, and dined with a rich ship-builder at Saardam, whose name was Kalf, and the first who had traded to Petersburg. His son had lately arrived from France, whither Peter was going. The Czar and Czarina were greatly entertained with an adventure of this young man, which I now mention, only to shew the difference between the manners of that country and ours.

KALF had sent his son to Paris, to learn the French tongue, and was desirous that he should live in a genteel manner there, and had ordered him to lay aside the plain garb which the inhabitants of Saardam wear, and to provide himself with fashionable cloaths at Paris, and to live in a manner, rather suitable to his fortune than his education; he knew his son's disposition, that this indulgence would have no bad effect on his usual frugality and sobriety.

THE French word *Veau* being calf, our young traveller took the name of *De Veau*; and when he

† July 14. 1717.

came to Paris, he lived in a splendid manner, spent his money freely, and made several genteel connections. At Paris it is very common to bestow, without reserve, the title of count and marquis, whether a person has any claim to it, or not, if he is only a gentleman. This foolish practice has been allowed by the government, in order that, by thus confounding all ranks, and consequently humbling the nobility, there might be less danger of civil wars, which were formerly so frequent. In fine, the titles of marquis and count, without possessions agreeable to that dignity, are like those of knight, without being of any order; or abbe without any church preferment, are things of so small consequence, as not to affect a nation.

Mr. Kalf was always called the count de Veau by his friends and servants: he frequently supped with the princesses, and played at the duchess of Berry's; and few strangers were better received. A young nobleman, who had been always one of his companions in these parties of pleasure, engaged to pay him a visit at Saardam, and did so. When he arrived at the village, he enquired for the house of count Kalf; when being shewn into a ship builder's yard, he found there the young count, dressed in a jacket and trowsers, after the Dutch fashion, with an ax in his hand, overseeing his father's workmen. He was received by count Kalf in that plain manner to which he had been accustomed from his birth, and from which he never departed.

parted. The good-natured reader will forgive this little digreſſion, as it is a ſatire on vanity, and a panegyric on true virtue.

THE Czar continued three months in Holland, during which his time was employed in more ſerious affairs than count Kalf's adventure. Since the treaties of Nimeguen, Ryſwick, and Utrecht, the Hague had been reckoned the center of negotiations in Europe. This little city, or rather village, the moſt pleaſant of any in the north, is chiefly inhabited by foreign miniſters, and travellers, who come for inſtruction to this univerſal academy. A great revolution in Europe was then in agitation. The Czar having got intelligence of the approaching ſtorm, prolonged his ſtay in the Netherlands, that he might be nearer at hand, to obſerve the intrigues going forward, both in the north and ſouth, and prepare himſelf for the part it would be proper for him to act.

CHAP.

CHAP. VIII.

Continuation of the travels of Peter the Great. Goertz's conspiracy. Reception of Peter in France.

PETER easily perceived that his allies were jealous of his power, and found that there is sometimes more difficulty with friends than with enemies.

MECKLENBURG was one of the principal causes of those animosities, which almost always subsist between neigbbouring princes, who share in conquests. Peter was not willing that the Danes should have Wismar for themselves, and still less that they should demolish the fortifications, and yet they had done both.

HE openly protected the duke of Mecklenburg against the nobility of the country, and the king of England as openly protected the latter. On the other hand, he was greatly discontented with the king of Poland, or rather with the minister, count Fleming, who wanted to throw off that dependance on the Czar, which necessity and gratitude had imposed.

THE courts of England, Poland, Denmark, Holstein, Meclenburg, and Brandenburg, were distracted with intrigues and cabals.

Towards the end of the year 1716, and beginning of 1717, Goertz, who, as Baffewitz tells us in his memoirs, was weary of having only the title of counfellor of Holftein, and being on'y private plenipotentiary to Charles XII was the chief promoter of thefe commotions, with which he intended to difturb the peace of all Europe. His defign was to bring Charles XII. and the Czar together, not only with a view to finifh the war between them, but to unite them in friendfhip, to replace Staniflaus on the crown of Poland, and to wreft Bremen and Verden out of the hands of George I. king of England, and even to drive that prince from the Britifh throne, which would put it out of his power to aggrandife himfelf with any part of the dominions of Charles XII.

There was at the fame time a minifter of his own ftamp, who aimed at the overturning the kingdoms of England and France: this was cardinal Alberoni, who had more power at that time in Spain, than Goertz had in Sweden; a man of as audacious and enterprifing a fpirit as himfelf, but much more powerful, as being at the head of affairs, in a kingdom infinitely more rich, and who never paid his creatures and dependents in copper money.

Goertz, from the banks of the Baltic Sea, foon formed a connection with the court of Madrid. The cardinal and he both held a correfpondence with all the wandering Englifh who were friends of the houfe of Stuart. Goertz made vifits to every place where he thought he was likely to find any enemies

nemies of king George, and went succeſſively to Germany, Holland, Flanders, and Lorrain, and at laſt came to Paris, about the end of the year 1716. Cardinal Alberoni began by ſending to him, in Paris, a million of French livres, in order, to uſe the cardinal's own expreſſion, that he might begin to ſet fire to the train.

GOERTZ propoſed, that Charles XII. ſhould yield up ſeveral places to Peter, in order to enable him to recover all the others from his enemies, and that he might be at liberty to make a deſcent in Scotland, while the partiſans of the Stuart family ſhould raiſe a rebellion in England. After their former vain attempts to effect thoſe views, it was neceſſary to deprive the king of England of his chief ſupport, which at that time was the regent of France. It was certainly very extraordinary, to ſee France in league with England, againſt the grandſon of Lewis XIV. whom ſhe herſelf had placed on the throne of Spain, at the expence of her blood and treaſure, notwithſtanding the ſtrong confederacy formed to oppoſe him; but it muſt be conſidered, that at this time every thing was out of its natural courſe, and the intereſts of the regent were not thoſe of the kingdom. Alberoni, at that time, was carrying on a confederacy in France againſt this very regent. And the foundations of this grand project were laid almoſt as ſoon as the plan itſelf had been formed. Goertz was the firſt who was let into the ſecret, and was to have made a journey into Italy in diſguiſe, to hold a conference with the pretender, in the neighbourhood of Rome; from thence

thence he was to have haftened to the Hague, to have an interview with the Czar, and then to have finifhed the whole with the king of Sweden.

The writer of this hiftory is particularly well informed of every thing here advanced ; for baron Goertz propofed to him to accompany him in thefe journeys ; and notwithftanding he was very young at that time, he was one of the firft who knew any thing of thefe intrigues.

Goertz returned to Holland in the latter part of 1716, furnifhed with bills of exchange from cardinal Alberoni, and credentials plenipotentiary from Charles XII. It is certain that the Jacobite party were to have made a rifing in England, while Charles, in his return from Norway, was to make a defcent in the North of Scotland. This prince, who had not been able to preferve his own dominions in Germany, was going to invade and overturn thofe of his neighbours ; and juft efcaped from his prifon in Turky, and from amidft the afhes of his own city of Stralfund, he would crown the fon of James II. in London, as he had placed Staniflaus on the throne of Poland at Warfaw.

The Czar, who underftood a part of Goertz's projects, waited for the unfolding of the reft, without concerning himfelf with them, as indeed he was a ftranger to feveral of them. He was as fond of great and extraordinary enterprizes as Charles XII. Goertz, or Alberoni ; but then it was as the founder of a ftate, a law giver, and a found politician ; and perhaps Alberoni, Goertz, and even Charles himfelf, were turbulent men, rather than

perfons

persons of solid understanding, who took their measures with a just precaution; or perhaps after all, their ill successes may have subjected them to the charge of rashness and imprudence.

When Goertz was at the Hague, the Czar did not see him, as it would have given too much umbrage to the States Generals, who were in close alliance with, and attached to the party of the king of England; and even his ministers visited him only in private, and with great precaution, having orders from their master to hear all he had to offer, and to flatter him with hopes, without involving him in any engagement, or making use of the Czar's name in their conferences. But notwithstanding all these precautions, those who understood the nature of affairs plainly saw by his inactivity, when he might have made a descent upon Scania with the joint fleets of Russia and Denmark, by his visible coolness towards his allies, and the little regard he paid to their complaints, and lastly, by this journey of his, that there was a great change in affairs, which would very soon break out.

In the month of January 1717, a Swedish packet-boat, which was carrying letters over to Holland, being forced by a storm upon the coast of Norway, put into harbour there. The letters were seized, and those of baron de Goertz and some other public ministers being opened, furnished sufficient evidence of the northern revolution. The court of Denmark communicated these letters to the English ministry, who gave orders for arresting the Swedish minister Gillemburg then at the court of London, and seizing his papers; upon examining which they discovered part of his correspondence with the Jacobites.

KING George immediately wrote to the States-Generals *, requiring them to cause the person of baron Goertz to be arrested, agreeable to the treaty of union subsisting between England and that republic for their mutual security. But this minister, who had his creatures and emissaries in every part, was quickly informed of this order; upon which he instantly quitted the Hague, and was got as far as Arnheim, a town on the frontiers, when the officers and guards, who were in pursuit of him, and who are seldom accustomed to use such diligence in that country, came up with and took him, together with all his papers. He was strictly confined and treated with some indignities: and secretary Stank, the person who had counterfeited the signal manual of the young duke of Holstein in the affair of Toningen, was used worse. In short, the count of Gillemburg, the Swedish envoy to the court of Great Britain, and the baron de Goertz, minister plenipotentiary from Charles XII. were examined like two criminals, the one at London, and the other at Arnheim, while all the foreign ministers exclaimed against this procedure as a violation of the law of nations.

THIS privilege, which is more insisted upon than understood, and whose extent and limits have never yet been fixed, has in almost every age suffered ma-

* Feb. 1717.

ny violations. Several ministers have been ordered from the courts where they resided in a public character, and even their persons have been more than once seized upon, but this was the first instance of foreign ministers being interrogated at the bar of a court of justice, as if they were natives of the country. The court of London and the States Generals laid aside all rules upon seeing the danger that threatened the house of Hanover; but, in fact, this danger, when once discovered, ceased to be any longer danger, at least at that juncture.

The historian Norberg must have been very ill informed, or have had a very indifferent knowledge of men and things, or at least been strangely blinded by partiality, or under severe restrictions from his own court, to endeavour to persuade his readers, that the king of Sweden was not very deep in this conspiracy.

The affront offered to his ministers fixed Charles more than ever in his resolution to try every means to dethrone the king of England. But he found it necessary to dissemble once in his life-time. He disowned his ministers and their proceedings both to the regent of France and the States Generals, from the former of whom he raised a subsidy, and with the latter it was for his interest to preserve a good understanding. He did not however give king George so much satisfaction. His ministers Goertz and Gillemberg were kept six months in confinement, and this repeated insult confirmed him in his projects of revenge.

Peter, in the midst of all these alarms and jealousies,

lousies, avoided all engagements, waiting with patience the event of all from time; and having established such good order throughout his vast dominions, as that he had nothing to fear either at home or from abroad, he resolved to visit France. As he did not understand the French language, he was deprived of a great part of the advantage he might have reaped from his journey; but he thought there might be something there worthy observation, and had a mind to be a near witness of the terms on which the regent stood with the king of England, and whether that prince was staunch to his alliance.

Peter the Great was received in France as such a monarch ought to be. Marshal Tesse was sent to meet him, with a number of the principal lords of the court, a company of guards, and the king's coaches; but he travelled with such expedition, that he was at Gourney when the equipages arrived at Elbeuf. Entertainments were made for him in every place on the road, where his expedition would allow him to partake of them. On his arrival he was received in the Louvre, where the royal apartments were prepared for him, and others for the princes Kourakin and Dolgorouki, the vice chancellor Shaffiroff, the ambassador Tolstoy, the same who had suffered in his person that notorious violation of the laws of nations in Turky, and for the rest of his retinue. Orders were given for lodging and entertaining him in the most splendid and sumptuous manner. But Peter, who was come only to see what might be of use to him, and not to suffer

these

these ceremonious triflings, which were a restraint upon his natural plainness, and consumed a time that was precious to him, went the same evening to take up his lodging at the other end of the city, in the Hotel of Lesdiguiere, belonging to the Marshal Villeroi, where he was treated in the same manner as he would have been at the Louvre. The next day the regent of France paid him a visit in his hotel †, and the day afterwards the young king, then an infant, was brought to him led by his governor the Marshal de Villeroi, whose father had been governor to Lewis XIV. The Czar was carefully saved the trouble of returning this visit till two days after, when he received the compliments of the city of Paris. The second night he went to visit the king: the household troops were all under arms, and the young prince was brought to the Czar's coach. Peter, surprized and uneasy at the prodigious concourse of people assembled about the royal child, took him in his arms, and carried him for some time in that manner.

Some ministers, of more cunning than judgment, have pretended in their writings, that marshal Villeroi wanted to make the young king of France take the upper hand on this occasion, and that the Czar made use of this stratagem to overturn the ceremonial under the appearance of good nature and tenderness; but this notion is equally false and absurd. The natural good breeding of the French court, and the respect due to the person of Peter the Great,

† May 8 1717.

would not permit a thought of turning the honours intended him into an affront. The ceremonial confifted in doing every thing for a great monarch and a great man, that he himfelf could have defired, if he had given any attention to matters of this kind. The journeys of the emperors Charles IV. Sigifmund, and Charles V. to France, were by no means comparable, in point of fplendor, to this of Peter the Great. They vifited this kingdom only from motives of political intereft, and at a time when the arts and fciences, as yet in their infancy, could not render the æra of their journey fo memorable: but when Peter the Great, on his going to dine with the duke d'Antin in the palace of Petitbourg, about three leagues out of Paris, faw his own picture, which had been drawn for the occafion, brought on a fudden, and placed in a room where he was, he then found that no people in the world knew fo well how to receive fuch a gueft as the French.

He was ftill more furprifed, when, going to fee them ftrike the medals in the long gallery of the Louvre, where all the king's artifts have fuch elegant apartments; a medal which they were then ftriking happening to fall to the ground, the Czar ftooped haftily down to take it up, when he beheld his own head engraved thereon, and on the reverfe a Fame ftanding with one foot upon a globe, and underneath thefe words from Virgil, " Vires acquirit eundo;" a delicate and noble allufion, and equally adapted to his travels and his reputation. Several of thefe medals in gold were prefented to him,

him, and to all those who attended him. Wherever he went to view the works of any artists, they laid the master-pieces of their performances at his feet, which they besought him to accept. And when he went to see the tapestry of the Gobelins, the working-rooms of the king's statuaries, painters, goldsmiths, jewellers, or mathematical instrument-makers, whatever seemed to strike his eye, were always offered him in the king's name.

PETER, being a mechanic, an artist, and a geometrician, went to visit the academy of sciences, who honoured him with an exhibition of their most striking rarities; but he was the greatest rarity himself. With his own hand he corrected several geographical errors in the charts of his own dominions, and especially in those of the Caspian sea. In short, he condescended to become one of the members of that academy, and afterwards continued a correspondence in experiments and discoveries with that illustrious body. To find such travellers as Peter, we must go back to the times of a Pythagoras and an Anacharsis; and even they did not quit the command of a mighty empire, to improve their knowledge.

THE reader I suppose will not be offended at being told of the transport with which Peter the Great was seized on viewing the monument of cardinal Richlieu. Regardless of the beauties of the sculpture, which is a master-piece of its kind, he only admired the image of a minister who had rendered himself famous throughout Europe by the disturbance he raised, and restoring to France that glory which she had lost after the death of Henry IV. It is well known, that, embracing the statue with rapture, he burst forth into this exclamation: " Great man! I would have bestowed one half of my empire on thee, to have taught me to govern the other." And now, before he left Paris, he was desirous to see the famous Madam de Maintenon, whom he knew to be the real widow of Lewis XIV. and who was now drawing near her end. The conformity of the marriage of Lewis XIV. and his had raised an eager curiosity in him; but he had married an heroine, and Lewis only an agreeable wife.

He did not take the Czarina with him in this journey; he was apprehensive that the excess of ceremony would be troublesome to her, as well as the curiosity of a court, little qualified to make a proper estimate of the true merit of a woman, who from the banks of the Pruth to the coast of Finland, had, at the side of her husband, faced death both by sea and land.

CHAP.

CHAP. IX.

Of the return of the Czar to his dominions. Of his policy and occupations.

THE procedure of the Sorbonne to Peter when he went to visit the mausoleum of cardinal Richlieu, deserves to be treated of by itself.

Some doctors of the Sorbonne wanted to have the glory of bringing about an union between the Greek and Latin churches. Those who are acquainted with antiquity need not be told, that the Christian religion was brought into the West by the Asiatic Greeks; that it was of Eastern origin, and that the first fathers, the first councils, the first liturgies, and the first rites, were all from the East; that there is not a single title or office in the hierarchy, but was in Greek, and thereby plainly shews the source from whence we derive our religion. Upon the division of the Roman empire, it was natural to expect, that sooner or later there must be two religions as well as two empires, and that the same schism should arise between the eastern and western Christians, as between the Turks and Persians.

This schism certain doctors of the Sorbonne thought to crush all at once by means of a memorial which they presented to Peter the Great, and

effect

effect what Pope Leo IX and his succeffors, had in vain laboured for many ages to bring about, by legates, councils, and even money. These doctors should have known, that Peter the Great, who was the chief of the Ruffian church, was not likely to acknowledge the pope's authority. They expatiated in their memorial on the liberties of the Gallican church, which the Czar gave himself no concern about. They afferted that the popes ought to be subject to the councils, and that a papal decree is not an article of faith: but their reprefentations were in vain; all they got for their pains, was to make the pope their enemy by fuch free declarations, at the fame time that they pleafed neither the emperor nor the Ruffian church.

In this plan of union there were certain political objects, which the good fathers did not underftand, and fome points of controverfy which they pretended to underftand, and which each party explained according to the humour they were in. It was concerning the Holy Ghoft, which, according to the Latin church, proceeds from the Father and the Son, and which at prefent, according to the Greeks, proceeds from the Father through the Son, after having for a confiderable time proceeded from the Father only: on this occafion they quoted a paffage in St. Epiphanius, where it is faid, "that the Holy Ghoft is neither brother to the Son, nor the Father's grandfon."

But Peter, when he left Paris, had other bufinefs to mind, than that of explaining paffages in St. Epiphanius. Neverthelefs, he received the memorial

morial of the Sorbonne with great affability. That learned body wrote to some of the Russian bishops, who returned a polite answer, though the major part of them were offended at the proposed union. It was in order to remove any apprehensions of such an union, that Peter, some time afterwards, namely in 1718, when he had driven the Jesuits out of his dominions, instituted the ceremony of a burlesque conclave.

There was at this court an old fool, named Jotof, who had taught him to write, and who thought he had, by that trivial service, merited the highest honours and most important post. Peter, who sometimes softened the toils of government, by indulging his people in amusements, which was very proper for a nation not entirely reformed, promised his writing-master, to bestow on him one of the highest dignities in the world; accordingly, he appointed him knés papa, or supreme pontiff, with an appointment of two thousand rubles, and assigned him a house to live in, in the Tartarian ward at Petersburg. He was installed by a number of buffoons, with great ceremony, and four fellows who stammered were appointed to harangue him on his exaltation. He created a number of cardinals, and marched in procession at their head, and every member of the sacred college was made drunk with brandy. After the death of this Jotof, an officer, named Buturlin, succeeded him in this dignity. Moscow and Petersburg have three times seen this ridiculous ceremony, the absurdity of which, tho' it appeared of no moment, yet has, by its ridiculousness,

ness, confirmed the people in their aversion to a church, which pretended to the supreme power, and whose church had anathematised so many crowned heads. In this manner did the Czar revenge the cause of twenty emperors of Germany, ten kings of France, and a number of other sovereigns; and this was all the advantage the Sorbonne gained from its foolish attempt to unite the Latin and Greek churches.

The Czar's journey to France proved more beneficial to his kingdom, by bringing about a connection with a trading and industrious people, than by the projected union between two rival churches; one of which will always maintain its ancient independence, and the other its modern superiority.

Peter carried several artists with him out of France, in the same manner as he had done out of England; for every nation which he visited thought it an honour to assist him in his design of introducing the arts and sciences into his new formed state, and to be serviceable in this creation.

At this time, he drew up a sketch of a treaty of commerce with France, and which he put into the hands of his ministers at Holland, as soon as he returned thither, but was not signed by Chateauneuf till the fifteenth of August 1717, at the Hague. This treaty, besides having a respect to trade, was designed to bring about peace in the north. The king of France and the elector of Brandenburg accepted of the office of mediators, which Peter offered them. This was sufficient to give the king of England to understand, that the Czar was not well pleased

pleased with him, and raised the hopes of baron Goertz, who, from that time, exerted himself to bring about an union between Charles and Peter, to stir up new enemies against George the First, and to assist cardinal Alberoni in his schemes in every part of Europe. Goertz now paid and received visits publicly from the Czar's ministers at the Hague, to whom he notified, that he was invested with full power from Sweden to conclude a peace.

The Czar suffered Goertz to dispose all his batteries, not giving the least assistance himself therein, and was prepared either to make peace with the king of Sweden, or to carry on the war, and continued still in alliance with the kings of Denmark, Poland, and Prussia, and in appearance with the elector of Hanover.

It appears plain, that he had no fixed design, but that of profiting by every conjuncture and circumstance, and that his main view was to compleat all the new establishments he had set on foot. He well knew, that the negotiations and interests of princes, their leagues, their friendships, their jealousies, and their enmities, were subject to change with each revolving year, and that frequently not the smallest traces remain of the greatest political efforts. A single manufactory, well founded, is often of more real advantage to a state than twenty treaties.

Peter having rejoined his consort, who was waiting for him in Holland, continued his travels with her. They crossed Westphalia, and arrived at Berlin in a private manner. The new king of

Prussia

Prussia was as much an enemy to ceremonious vanities, and the pomp of a court, as the Russian monarch; and it was an instructive lesson to the *etiquette* of Vienna and Spain, the *punctilio* of Italy, and the *politesse* of the French court, to see a king, in a wooden elbow-chair, who was clothed as a common soldier, and who had banished from his table, not only all the luxuries, but even the more moderate conveniencies of life.

The Czar and Czarina observed the same plain manner of living; and had Charles XII. been with them, the world might have beheld our crowned heads, with less pomp and state about them, than a German bishop, or a cardinal of Rome. Never were luxury and effeminacy opposed by such noble examples.

It must be owned, that if one of our fellow subjects had, from mere curiosity, made the fifth part of the journeys that Peter did for the good of his kingdom, he would have been looked upon as a very extraordinary person. From Berlin he went to Dantzick, still accompanied by his wife, and from thence to Mittau, where he protected his niece, the duchess of Courland, lately become a widow. He visited all the places he had conquered; in Petersburg he made many new and useful regulations; from thence he goes to Moscow, where he gave orders for rebuilding all the houses of private persons that had fallen to ruin; from thence he transports himself to Czaritsin, on the river Wolga, to stop the incursions of the Cuban Tartars; constructs lines of communication from the Wolga to the Don, and erects

erects forts at certain distances, between the two rivers. At the same time he caused the military code, which he had lately composed, to be printed, and erected a court of justice, to examine into the conduct of his ministers, and for rectifying abuses in his finances. He pardons several who were found guilty, and punishes others. Among the latter was the great prince Menzikoff himself, who stood in need of the royal clemency. But a more rigorous sentence, which he thought himself obliged to utter against his own son, filled the whole empire with distress, and a glorious life with affliction.

CHAP. X.

Trial and condemnation of prince Alexis Petrowitz.

PETER the Great, when only seventeen years of age, married, in the year 1689, Eudocia Theodora, or Theodorouna Lapoukin. Bred up in the prejudices of her country, and incapable of surmounting them like her husband, the greatest opposition he met with in erecting his empire, and forming his people, came from his wife: she was, as it is too common for her sex, a slave to superstition; every new and useful alteration she looked upon as a species of sacrilege; and every foreigner, whom the Czar employed in the prosecution of his schemes, she looked upon as corruptors and innovators.

The openness of her complaints gave encouragement to the factious, and those who were the advocates for ancient customs and manners. Her conduct, in other respects, by no means made amends for such heavy imperfections. The Czar was at length obliged to repudiate her in 1696, and shut her up in a convent at Susdal, where they obliged her to take the veil under the name of Helen.

The son, whom he had by her in 1690, brought into the world with him the same unhappy disposition of his mother, and that disposition received additional strength from the first elements of his education. My memoirs say, that he was entrusted to the care of superstitious men, who vitiated his mind. It was in vain that they hoped to correct these first impressions, by giving him foreign preceptors; for he hated them. He was not born destitute of genius; he spoke and wrote German well; he had a good notion of drawing, and had made some progress in the mathematics: but these very memoirs with which I am intrusted affirm, that the reading of ecclesiastical books was the ruin of him. The young Alexis imagined he saw in these books a condemnation of every thing which his father had done. There were some priests at the head of the malecontents, and by the priests he suffered himself to be governed.

They persuaded him that the whole nation abhorred his father's projects; that the frequent indispositions of the Czar prognosticated but a short life; and that his son could not hope to please the nation,

nation, but by testifying his aversion for all changes of custom. These murmurs, and these counsels, did not break out into an open faction or conspiracy; but every thing seemed to tend that way, and the tempers of the public were inflamed.

WHAT put the young prince most out of humour, was his father's marriage with Catherine in 1707, and the children which he had by her. Peter tried every method to reclaim him; he even placed him at the head of a regency for a year; he sent him to travel; he married him in 1711, at the end of the campaign of Pruth, to the princess of Brunswick. This marriage was attended with great misfortunes. Alexis, now twenty years old, gave himself up to the debauchery of youth, and that boorishness of ancient manners he so much delighted in. These irregularities almost brutalized him. His wife, despised, ill-treated, wanting even necessaries, and deprived of all comfort, lingered in affliction, which put an end to her life, November the fourth, 1715.

SHE left the prince Alexis one son; and according to the natural order, this son was one day to become heir to the empire. Peter perceived with sorrow, that, on his decease, all his labours were likely to be destroyed by his own son. After the death of the princess he wrote a letter to his son, equally tender and resolute: it finished with these words: "I will wait a little time, to see if you will amend yourself, if not, know that I will cut you off from the succession, as we lop off an useless member. Do not imagine, that I mean only to frighten

frighten you ; do not rely upon the title of being my only son ; for, if I spare not my own life for my country, and the good of my people, how shall I spare you ? I will rather chuse to leave my kingdom to a stranger who deserves it, than to my own undeserving offspring "

THIS is the letter of a father, but it is still more the letter of a legislator ; it shews us besides, that the order of succession was not invariably established in Russia, as in other kingdoms, by those fundamental laws by which parents cannot exclude their children, and the Czar thought he had an undoubted right to dispose of an empire which he had founded.

AT this very time the empress Catherine was brought-to-bed of a prince, who died afterwards in 1719. Whether this news sunk the courage of Alexis, or whether it was imprudence or bad counsel, he wrote to his father, that he renounced the crown, and all hopes of reigning. " God is my witness, said he, and I swear by my soul, that I will never pretend to the succession I put my children into your hands, and I desire only a provision for life."

THE Czar wrote him a second letter as follows: " You speak of the succession, as if I stood in need of your consent in the disposal thereof. I reproached you with the aversion you have shewn to all kind of business, and signified to you, that I was highly dissatisfied with your conduct in general; but to these particulars you have given me no answer. Paternal exhortations make no impression on you,

you, wherefore I resolve to write you this once for the last time. If you despise the advices I give you while I am alive, what regard will you pay to them after my death? but though you had the inclination at present to be true to your promises, yet those bushy beards will be able to wind you as they please, and force you to falsify them. They have no dependence but upon you. You have no sense of gratitude towards him who gave you life. Since you arrived at maturity, have you ever assisted him in toils and labours? Do you not censure and condemn, nay, even affect to hold in detestation, whatever I do for the good of my people? I have reason to believe, that if you survive me, you will overturn every thing that I have done. Take your choice, either endeavour to make yourself worthy of the succession, or turn monk. I expect your answer, either in writing, or personally, otherwise I shall treat you as a common malefactor."

This letter was very severe, and it was easy for the prince to have replied that he would alter his conduct; instead of which, he only returned a short answer to his father, desiring permission to turn monk.

This resolution appeared altogether unnatural; and it may furnish matter of surprize, that the Czar should think of travelling, and leaving a son at home so obstinate and ill-affected; but, at the same time, his doing so is next to a proof, that he thought he had no reason to apprehend a conspiracy from that son.

Peter, before he set out for Germany and France,

France, went to see his son. The prince, who was at that time ill, or at least feigned himself so, received his father in his bed, where he protested, with the most solemn oaths that he was ready to retire into a cloister. The Czar gave him six months to consider of it, and then set out on his travels with his consort.

He had scarce reached Copenhagen, when he heard that the Czarowitz conversed only with factious and evil-minded persons, who strove to feed his discontent. Upon this the Czar wrote to him, that he had only to chuse between a throne and a convent; and that, if he had any thoughts of succeeding him, he must immediately come to him at Copenhagen.

But the confidents of the prince endeavoured to persuade him how dangerous it would be to trust himself in a place where he could have no friends to advise him, and where he was to be exposed to the anger of an incensed father, and a mother-in-law without affection; he, under pretence of going to join his father at Copenhagen, took the road to Vienna, and threw himself under the protection of the emperor Charles VI. his brother-in-law, designing to stay at his court till the death of the Czar.

This adventure of Alexis was nearly the same as that of Lewis XI. of France, who, when he was dauphin, quitted the court of his father Charles VII. and took refuge with the duke of Burgundy. But Lewis was much more culpable than Alexis, as he married in direct opposition to his father's will,

raised

raised an army against him, and threw himself into the arms of a prince, who was Charles's natural enemy, and refused to hearken to the repeated instances of his father, to return back to his court.

THE Czarowitz, on the contrary, had married only in compliance with his father's orders, had never rebelled against him, nor raised an army, nor taken refuge in the dominions of an enemy, and returned to throw himself at his feet, upon the very last letter he received from him: for, as soon as Peter knew that his son had been at Vienna, and had afterwards retired to Tyrol, and from thence to Naples, which, at that time, belonged to the emperor, he dispatched Romanzoff, a captain of his guards, and the privy counsellor Tolstoy, with a letter written with his own hand, and dated at Spa, the twenty-first of July, N. S. 1717. They found the prince at Naples, in the castle of St. Elme, and delivered him his father's letter, which was as follows:

" I NOW write to you for the last time, to let you know, that you must instantly comply with my orders, which will be communicated to you by Tolstoy and Romanzoff. On your obedience, I give you my sacred word and promise, that I will not punish you; and that if you will return home, I will love you better than ever; but, if you do not, I, as your father, and in virtue of the authority which God has given me over you, denounce against you my eternal curse: and, as your sovereign, declare to you, that I will find ways to punish you, in which I trust God himself will assist me, me, and espouse the cause of an injured parent and king.

REMEMBER that I have never laid any restraint upon you. Was I obliged to leave you at liberty to chuse your own way of life? Had I not the power in my own hands to oblige you to conform to my will? I had only to command and make myself obeyed."

THE viceroy of Naples easily persuaded Alexis to return to his father. This is an incontestible proof that the emperor of Germany had no intentions to enter into any engagements with the prince that might give umbrage to his father. Alexis therefore returned with the envoys, bringing with him his mistress Aphrosyne.

THE Czarowitz in all this may be considered as an ill advised young man, who had gone to Vienna, and to Naples, instead of going to Copenhagen, agreeable to the orders of his father and sovereign. Had he been guilty of no other fault than this, which is common to young people, it was certainly very excusable. The prince determined to return to his father, on the faith of his having taken God to witness, that he not only would pardon him, but that he would love him better than ever. But it appears by the instructions given to the two envoys who went to fetch him back, and even by the Czar's own letter, that his father required him to confess the persons who had been his advisers, and also to fulfil the oath he made of renouncing the succession.

IT seems difficult to reconcile this exclusion of
the

the Czarewitz from the fucceffion, with the other part of the oath by which the Czar had bound himfelf in his letter, namely, that of loving him better than ever. Perhaps, divided between paternal love, and the juftice he owed to himfelf and people, as a fovereign, he might limit the renewal of his love to his fon in a convent, inftead of that to a fon on a throne; perhaps likewife, he was in hopes to reduce him to reafon, and render him worthy of the fucceffion at laft, by making him fenfible of the lofs of a crown which he had forfeited by his own indifcretion. In fuch a critical, intricate, and afflicting affair, it may be eafily fuppofed that the minds of both father and fon were too much agitated to reft in any fixed determination.

The prince arrived at Mofcow on the thirteenth of February N. S. 717, and the fame day went to throw himfelf at the knees of his father. They had a long difcourfe together, and a report was immediately fpread through the city, that the father and fon were reconciled, and that all paft tranfactions were buried in oblivion. But the next day, orders were iffued for the regiments of guards to be under arms at break of day, and for all the Czar's minifters, boyars, and counfellors, to repair to the great hall of the caftle; as alfo for the prelates, together with two monks of St. Bafil, profeffors of divinity, to affemble in the cathedral at the tolling of the great bell. The unhappy prince was then conducted, without a fword, into the great caftle like a prifoner, and being come in his father's prefence, threw himfelf in tears at his feet,

F 2 and

and prefented him a writing, containing a confeſſion of his faults, declaring himſelf unworthy of the ſucceſſion, and begs only that his life might be ſpared

The Czar, raiſing up his ſon, withdrew with him into a private room, where he put many queſtions to him, declaring to him at the ſame time, that if he concealed any one circumſtance relating to his elopement, his head ſhould anſwer for it. The prince was then brought back to the great hall, where the council was aſſembled, and the Czar's declaration, which had been previouſly prepared, was publicly read in his preſence.

In this piece the father reproaches his ſon with all thoſe faults we have before related, namely, his little application to ſtudy, his connexions with the favourers of the antient cuſtoms and manners of the country, and his ill behaviour to his wife. "He has even violated the conjugal faith (faith the Czar in his manifeſto) by giving his affection to a proſtitute of the moſt ſervile and low condition, during the life-time of his lawful ſpouſe." It is certain that Peter himſelf had repudiated his own wife in favour of a captive; but that captive was a perſon of exemplary merit, and that the Czar had juſt cauſe for diſcontent againſt his wife, who was at the ſame time his ſubject. The Czarowitz, on the contrary, had abandoned his princeſs for a young woman, hardly known to any one, and who had no other merit but that of her beauty. So far there appears ſome errors of a young man, whom a parent ought to reprove, and may pardon his ſon.

He

He next reproaches his son with his flight to Vienna, and his having put himself under the emperor's protection; he adds, that "he had calumniated his father, by telling the emperor that he was persecuted by him; and lastly, that he had made intercession with the emperor to assist him with an armed force.

We cannot easily conceive that the emperor could with any propriety enter into a war with the Czar on such an occasion; nor could he have interposed otherwise between an incensed father and a disobedient son, than by his good offices, to promote a reconciliation. Accordingly we find, that Charles VI. had only entertained the prince, and on the Czar's demanding him he was sent back.

Peter adds, in this terrible piece, that Alexis had persuaded the emperor, "that he went in danger of his life," if he returned back to Russia. Surely it was in some measure justifying these complaints of the prince, to condemn him to death at his return, and especially after so solemn a promise to pardon him; but we shall see in the course of this history what moved the Czar to pass such a singular sentence. In short, an absolute sovereign was here seen pleading against his son.

"In this manner, says he, has our son returned; and although his flight deserved to be punished with death, yet out of our fatherly affection we pardon his crimes; but considering his notorious unworthiness and immorality, we cannot in conscience leave him the succession to the empire;

it being too manifest, that by his vicious courses he would be subverted, so as too occasion the loss of all the provinces, which would be much to be pitied.

Our faithful subjects, if by such a successor, we should throw into a condition much worse than any they were in before; according to our paternal power, and, in quality of sovereign prince, and according to the laws of our empire, we deprive our said son Alexis, for his crimes and unworthiness, of the succession after us to our throne of Russia, even though not a single person of our family should exist at the time of our death.

And we constitute, appoint and declare successor to the said throne after us, our second son Peter *, though yet very young, having no successor that is older.

We lay on our said son Alexis our paternal curse, if he shall claim the said succession, or use any means to procure it.

And we require our faithful subjects, whether ecclesiastics or seculars, of every rank and condition, and the whole Russian nation, in pursuance to this appointment and our will, to acknowledge and consider our said son Peter nominated by us as our lawful successor, and agreeably to this present ordonnance, to confirm the whole by oath before the holy altar, upon the holy gospels, and kissing the cross.

* This was the son of the empress Catherine, who died April 15. 1719.

AND

AND as those who shall at any time whatever oppose this our will, and who from the date hereof shall dare to consider our son Alexis as successor, or assist him for that purpose, we declare them traitors to us and their country. And we have ordered these presents to be every where published, signed with our hand, and sealed with our seal, that no person may pretend ignorance. Given at Moscow the thirteenth of February, N. S. 1718.

It would seem that these instruments were got in readiness, or at least drawn up with amazing dispatch; for the Czarowitz did not return to Moscow till the thirteenth of February, and his disinheritance in favour of the empress Catherine's son is dated the fourteenth.

THE prince on his side signed the renunciation of the succession, whereby " he acknowledges his exclusion to be just, as having merited it by his own fault and unworthiness; and I do hereby swear (adds he) in the name of the sacred and almighty Trinity, to submit myself in all things to my father's will, &c."

THESE instruments being signed, the Czar proceeded to the cathedral, where they were read a second time, and the whole body of the ecclesiastics signed their approbation with their seals at the bottom, to a copy prepared for that purpose. Never was a prince disinherited in so authentic a manner. There are many states where such an act would be of no validity; but in Russia, as in ancient Rome, every father could disinherit his son, and this power was still stronger in a sovereign than in a subject, and especially in such a sovereign as Peter.

It was however to be apprehended, that those very persons who had encouraged the prince against his father, and had advised him to withdraw himself from his court, might one day endeavour to overthrow a renunciation which had been imposed by force, and restore to the eldest son the crown which had been violently placed on the head of a younger brother by a second marriage. In such a case it was easy to foresee the certain consequence would be a civil war, and this would occasion the loss of the great and useful projects which Peter had so much laboured to establish; and therefore the present matter in question was to determine between the welfare of near eighteen millions of men (the number that the empire of Russia contained at that time) and the interest of a single person not capable of governing. It was therefore of the highest importance to know who were disaffected; and accordingly the Czar a second time threatened his son with capital punishment should he conceal any thing from him: and the prince was obliged to undergo a second examination by his father, and afterwards by commissioners appointed for that purpose.

One principal article that hastened his condemnation, was, a letter from M. Beyer, the emperor's resident at the court of Russia, dated at Petersburg, after the flight of the prince. The substance of this letter was, that the Russian army then assembled

at

at Mecklenburg had mutinied, and that several of the officers talked of clapping up Catherine and her son in the prison where the late empress whom Peter had repudiated, was confined, and of placing Alexis on the throne as soon as it could be found out where he was. This sedition fell to the ground, and there was not the least appearance that Alexis had ever countenanced it. A foreigner only spoke of it as a piece of news: the letter itself was not directed to prince Alexis, he had only a copy of it sent him from Vienna.

But a much heavier charge appeared against him, namely, the rough draught of a letter wrote with his own hand from Vienna, to the senators and prelates of Russia, in which were the following very strong assertions: "The continual injuries which I have undeservedly suffered, have at length obliged me to leave my country. I have narrowly escaped being confined in a convent, by those who have already served my mother in the same manner. I am now under the protection of a great prince, and I beseech you not to forsake me in this conjuncture.

The expression, *in this conjuncture*, which might have been looked on as seditious, appeared to have been blotted out, and then replaced again by his own hand, and afterwards effaced a second time; which shewed a young man under perturbation of mind, following the dictates of his resentment, and repenting of it at the very minute. There were only the rough draughts of these letters found; they never came to the persons they were designed for, the court of Vienna having taken care to stop them; a not inconsiderable proof that the emperor never intended to quarrel with the Czar, or to support the son against his father.

Several witnesses were brought to confront the prince; and one, named Afanassief, maintained, that he had formerly heard him mention, "I will say something to the bishops, who will say it again to the parish priests, they will tell it to their parishoners, and I shall be placed upon the throne whether I will or not."

Aphrosyne, his own mistress, was likewise brought to give evidence against him. The charge however was not well supported in its parts: there did not appear to have been any regular plan formed, any chain of intrigues, or any thing like a conspiracy or combination, or the least shadow of preparation for a change in the government. The whole affair was that of a son of a depraved and factious disposition, who thought himself injured by his father, and flying from him, and who wished for his death; but this son was heir to the greatest monarchy of our hemisphere, and in his situation no fault can be called small.

Besides his mistress's deposition, another witness was brought against him, in relation to the former Czarina his mother, and his sister the princess Mary. He was charged with having consulted his mother in regard to his flight, and having mentioned it to his sister. The bishop of Rostow, the confident of all three, having been seized, deposed that these two princesses, who were shut up in a convent, had intimated some hopes of a revolution in affairs that might restore them their liberty, and it was by their advice the prince had fled into Germany, instead of going to his father at Copenhagen. Their resentment being natural was the more dangerous, and what kind of a person this bishop of Rostow was, we shall learn at the end of this chapter.

ALEXIS at first denied several facts of this nature which were alledged against him, and by his very denials exposed himself to the punishment of death with which his father had threatned him, if he did not make a general and sincere confession.

AT length he acknowledged that several disrespectful words against his father, which were laid to his charge, had dropped from him, but excused himself by pleading passion and drunkenness.

THE Czar himself drew up several new interrogations. The fourth o which ran as follows:

"WHEN you saw by Beye's letter that there was a revolt among the troops in Mecklenburg, you seemed pleased with it; you must certainly have had some further views in this? and I believe you would have joined the rebels even in my lifetime?"

THIS was questioning the prince on the subject of his private thoughts, which, though they might be owned to a father, who by his counsels might rectify them, yet might they be concealed from a judge, as he is to determine only from attested facts. The private sentiments of a man's heart are not within the cognizance of a court of judicature, and the prince was at liberty either to deny or disguise them, being under no obligation to lay open his mind; yet we find him returning the following answer in writing: "Had the rebels invited me, during your life-time, I believe I should have joined them, if I had found them strong enough."

It can scarcely be thought, that of himself he should return such an answer; and it would be full as strange, according to the European custom, to condemn him for thoughts which he might have had in a case which did not happen.

To this strange confession of his secret thoughts, which had till then been concealed, were added proofs which would hardly be admitted in a court of justice in any other country.

The distressed prince, almost deprived of his senses, made an ingenuous confession of every thing which could help forward his destruction; and at length acknowledged, that in a private confession to the arch-priest James, he had accused himself before God, that he had wished for his father's death: and that his confessor made answer, "God will pardon you this wish; we all with the same."

Proofs resulting from private confession are not allowed by the canons of our church, inasmuch as they are between God and the penitent; and both the Greek and Latin churches are agreed, that this intimate and secret correspondence between a sinner and the Deity are beyond the cognizance of a temporal court of justice. But here the welfare of a state and the sovereign were concerned.

cerned. The arch-priest, being put to the torture, confirmed all that the prince had revealed, and this trial furnished the unprecedented instance of a confessor accused by his penitent, and the penitent by his mistress. To this may be added another singular circumstance, namely, that the archbishop of Rezan having been involved in several accusations on account of having spoken too favourably of the young Czarowitz in one of his sermons, at the time that his father's resentment first broke out against him; the prince declared in his answer to one of the interrogations, that he had depended on the assistance of that prelate, at the same time that he was at the head of the ecclesiastical court, which the Czar had consulted with regard to this criminal process against his son.

ANOTHER remark to be made in this extraordinary trial, which we find so very blindly related in the absurd history of Peter the Great by the pretended boyar Nesterfuranoy, is as follows;

IN Alexis's answers to the first question put to him by his father, he acknowledged, that while he was at Vienna, where he could not be admitted to see the emperor, he applied to count Schonborn the high chamberlain, who said to him, that "the emperor would not forsake him, and at a proper season, upon the death of his father, that he would assist him to recover the throne by force of arms." Upon which the prince made answer, "This is what I by no means ask: if the emperor will only grant me his protection for the present, I ask no more." This deposition is plain, natural, and carries

ries with it a great appearance of truth; for it would have been madness to have asked the emperor for troops to dethrone his father, and no body would have dared to have made such an absurd proposal, either to the emperor, prince Eugene, or to the council. This deposition was in the month of February; and four months after, on the first of July, towards the conclusion of the proceedings against the Czarowitz, that the prince is made to say, in the last answers he delivered in writing:

"INTENDING in nothing to imitate my father, I endeavoured to come at the succession by any means whatever, *excepting such as were just*. I was for having it by a foreign assistance; and had I succeeded and the emperor had fulfilled *what he had promised me*, to procure me the throne of Russia even by force of arms, I would have spared no pains to have got possession of it. For instance, if the emperor had asked me in return for his services, a body of my country troops to serve him against any power whatever, or a large sum of money to defray the charges of a war, I should have done every thing he asked, and would have bestowed magnificent presents on his ministers and generals. I would at my own expence have maintained the auxiliary troops he might have supplied me to get possession of the crown; and, in fine, I should have stuck at nothing to have accomplished my ends."

This answer of the prince seems greatly forced, and looks as if the unhappy deponent was exerting his utmost efforts to make himself guilty; nay, he

seems

seems to have spoken absolutely contrary to truth in a capital point He says the emperor had promised to procure him the crown by open force, which was false: Schonborn had given him hopes, that, after the death of the Czar, the emperor might assist him to recover his birth-right; but the emperor himself had never made him any promise. In a word, the case was not to rebel against his father, but to succeed him on his demise.

By this last deposition he says what he believes he should have done, had he been obliged to dispute his birth right, which he had not judicially renounced till after his journey to Vienna and Naples Now then we have a second deposition, not of what he had already done, and made himself obnoxious to the rigour of the laws, but of what he fancies he should have done, had occasion offered, and which of consequence comes not within the authority of any court of justice. Here we see him twice together accuse himself of secret thoughts that he might have had in a future time. The whole world does not produce one single instance of a man tried and condemned for vague and transitory ideas that came into his mind, and which he never communicated to any one. There is not one court of justice in Europe that would take notice of a man accusing himself of criminal thoughts; nay, we believe that they are not punished by God himself, unless accompanied by a fixed resolution to put them in practice.

To these considerations, however natural, it may be answered, that the Czarowitz, by his concealing several of the accomplices in his elopement, had given his father a just right to punish him. His pardon was annexed only on condition of making a full and open confession, which he did not make till it was too late. In fine, after so public an affair, it was not in human nature to expect Alexis should ever forgive a brother for whose sake he had been disinherited; therefore it was thought better to punish one guilty person, than to put a whole nation in danger, and herein the rigour of justice corresponded with reasons of state.

The manners and laws of one nation are not to be judged of by those of others. The Czar had the fatal, but incontestible right of punishing his son with death, merely for his elopement; and he thus expresses himself in his declaration to the judges and bishops "Though, according to all laws, civil and divine, and especially those of Russia, which grant an absolute jurisdiction to fathers over their children (even fathers in private life) we have a sufficient and absolute power to judge our son for his crimes according to our pleasure, without consulting any person, yet, as men not being so clear sighted in their own affairs, as in those of others, and as the most eminent and skilful physicians when sick call in the advice and assistance of others; so we being afraid of the dread majesty of heaven, and minding to keep our consciences as clear as in a solemn appeal to Almighty God, I have signed, and sworn, a promise of pardon to my son, in case he should declare to me the whole truth.

And though my son had broke his promise by concealing

concealing the most important circumstances of his rebellious designs against us, yet that we may not in any thing depart from obligations, we pray you to consider this affair with seriousness and attention, and see what punishment he has deserved. I desire neither favour nor partiality either to him or me; for should you think that he deserves but a slight punishment, it will not be disagreeable to me, for I swear to you by the great God and his judgments, that absolutely you have no consequences to apprehend from this.

NEITHER let it give you the least uneasiness, that you are to pass sentence on the son of your sovereign, but administer justice without respect of persons, and destroy not your own souls and mine also, by doing any thing to injure our country, or upbraid our consciences in the great and terrible day of judgment."

THE Czar made a declaration of the same kind to the clergy. Thus every thing was transacted with the greatest solemnity. Peter's behaviour through the whole of this affair was so undisguised, as shewed him to be fully satisfied of the justice of his cause.

THIS criminal process of the heir of so great an empire lasted from the end of February to the 5th of July N. S. The prince was several times examined, and made the confessions required, the most essential of which we have related.

ON the first of July the clergy delivered their opinion in writing. In fact, it was their opinion only, and not a judgment, which the Czar required of of them. The beginning is deserving of the attention of all Europe.

"This affair (say the bishops and the rest of the clergy) does in no wise belong to the ecclesiastical court, and the absolute power invested in the sovereign of the Russian empire, is subject to the cognizance of his subjects; but he has an unlimited power of acting herein as to him shall seem best, without any inferior having a right to intervene."

This preamble is succeeded by several texts of scripture, particularly Leviticus, wherein it is said, *cursed be he that curseth his father or mother;* and the gospel of St. Matthew, which repeats this severe denunciation. And they conclude, after several other citations, with these remarkable words.

"If his majesty is inclined to punish the delinquent according to his deeds and the measure of his guilt, he has before him examples from the Old Testament; if he is inclined to shew mercy, he has a pattern in our Lord Jesus Christ, who kindly receives the prodigal son, when returning with a contrite heart, who set free the woman taken in adultery, whom the law sentenced to be stoned to death, and who delights in mercy more than burnt offerings. He has the example of David, who spared his son Absalom, who had rebelled against him, saying to his captains when going forth to fight, *spare my son Absalom.* The father was here inclinable to mercy, but divine justice did not spare him.

"The

"THE heart of the Czar is in the hands of God; let him take that side to which it shall please the Almighty to incline him."

THIS memorial was signed by eight arch-bishops and bishops, four arch-priests, and two professors of divinity, and, as we have already noticed, the metropolitan arch-bishop of Rezan, who had been one of the prince's advisers, was the first that signed the memorial.

As soon as the clergy had signed this opinion, they presented it to the Czar. It is easy to observe that this body were inclined for mercy; and nothing can be more beautiful than the contrast between the mildness of Jesus Christ, and the rigour of the Jewish law, placed before the eyes of a father, who was trying his own son.

ALEXIS was examined the same day for the last time, and signed his final confession in writing, wherein he attests himself "to have frequented the company of priests and monks, to have drank intemperately with them, and to have received from their conversations the first impressions which made his mind abhor the duties of his station, and even created in him a hatred of his father."

IF he made this confession of his own accord, it shews that he knew nothing of the mild advice the body of clergy whom he thus accuses, had lately given his father; and is a strong proof how great a change the Czar had wrought in the manners of the clergy of his time, who, in so short a period were become capable of drawing up a writing, which for its wisdom and eloquence might have been owned

without

without a blush by the most illustrious fathers of the church, as at the beginning of Peter's reign, they were in a state of the most deplorable ignorance.

It is in this last confession that Alexis declares what we have already related, viz. that he endeavoured to secure to himself the succession *by any means whatever, except such as were just.*

It appears by this last confession, that the prince was afraid he had not rendered himself sufficiently criminal in the eyes of his judges, by his former self-accusations, and that, by saying he had a malignant mind, was a bad man, and imagining how he would have acted had he been the master, he was carefully labouring how to justify the fatal sentence of death which was about to be pronounced against him, and which was done on the 5th of July. This sentence will be found, at large, at the end of this history, therefore we shall only observe, that it begins like the opinion of the clergy, by declaring, that "it belongs not to subjects to take cognizance of such an affair, but to the sovereign alone, whose authority is derived from God;" and then, after having specified the several articles against the prince, the judges express themselves thus: "What shall we think of this intended rebellion, quite unparalleled in history, joined to the horror of a double parricide against him, who was his father and his sovereign?

It is probable these words have been wrong translated from the trial printed by order of the Czar; for certainly there have been instances in history

tory of much greater rebellions; and no part of the proceedings against the Czarowitz discover any design in him of killing his father. Perhaps, by the word *parricide*, is understood the deposition made by the prince, that one day he declared at confession, that he had wished his father's death, and consequently that of his sovereign. But, how can a private declaration of a secret thought, under the seal of confession, be a double parricide?

However it be, the Czarowitz was unanimously condemned to die, but no mention was made in the sentence of the manner in which he was to suffer. Of one hundred and forty four judges, there was not one thought of a lesser punishment than death. An English pamphlet, which made a great noise at that time, affirms, that if such a cause had been brought before an English parliament, there would not have been one judge who would have voted for the slightest penalty.

There cannot be a stronger proof of the difference of times and places. Manlius would have been condemned by the laws of England to lose his own life, for having put his son to death; yet he was admired and extolled for that action by the severe Romans: but the laws of England would not punish a prince of Wales for leaving the kingdom, who, as a peer of the realm, has a right to come and go when he pleases: but the laws of Russia do not permit the sovereign's son to depart the kingdom without his consent. A criminal thought, not carried into execution, is not punishable by the laws of England or France, but it is in Russia. A continued

tinued formal and repeated disobedience of commands would, amongst us, be considered only as a misconduct, which ought to be checked; but in Russia, it was judged a capital crime in the heir of a great empire, the ruin of which might have been the consequence of that disobedience. Lastly, the Czarowitz was guilty against the whole nation, by his design of throwing it back into that state of ignominy and ignorance from which his father had so lately raised it.

Such was the acknowledged power of the Czar, that he might put his son to death for disobedience, without consulting any other person; nevertheless, he submitted the case to the judgment of the representatives of the nation, so that it was the nation itself who passed sentence on the prince; and Peter, confident of the equity of his proceedings, caused the trial to be printed and translated into several languages, thus submitting himself to the judgment of the whole world.

The laws of history would not permit us to disguise or palliate any thing in the relation of this tragical event. Europe was divided in its sentiments, whether most to pity a young prince, accused by his own father, and condemned to death, by those who were one day to have been his subjects; or the father, who thought himself obliged to sacrifice his own son to the welfare of the empire.

It has been said by several writers, that the Czar sent to Spain for a copy of the proceedings against Don Carlos, who had been condemned to death by

Philip

Philip the second. But this is false, as Don Carlos was never brought to trial: the conduct of Peter I. was quite different from that of Philip. The Spaniard never made known to the world the reasons for which he had caused his son to be imprisoned, nor the manner of the prince's death. He wrote letters on this occasion to the Pope and the empress, which were absolutely contradictory to each other. William prince of Orange taxed Philip publicly of having sacrificed his son and his wife to his jealousy, and of having behaved rather like a jealous and cruel husband, and an unnatural and murdering father, than a severe and upright judge. Philip made no answer to this accusation against him. Peter, on the contrary, did nothing but in the eyes of the world; and openly declared, that he preferred his nation to his own son, submitting his cause to the judgment of the clergy and nobility of his kingdom, and made the whole world the judge of their proceedings and his own.

ANOTHER extraordinary circumstance attending this melancholy affair, is, that the empress Catherine, hated by the Czarowitz, and whom he had publicly threatened with the worst of treatment, whenever he should mount the throne, was not in the least accessary to his misfortunes; and was neither accused nor even suspected by any foreign minister residing at the court of Russia, of having taken the least step against a son-in-law, from whom she had every thing to fear. It is true, indeed, that no one pretends to say she interceded for his pardon: all the accounts of these times, and especially those of

the

the count de Baſſewitz, agree, that ſhe greatly pitied his misfortunes.

I HAVE before me the memoirs of a public miniſter, in which I find the following words: "I was preſent when the Czar ſaid to the duke of Holſtein, that the Czarina Catherine had intreated him to prevent the ſentence paſſed upon the Czarowitz being publicly read to that prince. "Content yourſelf, ſaid ſhe, with compelling him to become a monk; for this public and formal condemnation of your ſon will reflect an odium on your grandſon."

THE Czar, however, would not yield to the interceſſion of his conſort; but he thought there was a neceſſity to have the ſentence publicly read to the prince, in order that he might not have the leaſt pretence to diſpute this ſolemn act, in which he himſelf acquieſced, and that being dead in law, it would for ever diſable him from pretending to the crown.

NEVERTHELESS, if, after the death of Peter, a powerful party had aroſe in favour of Alexis, would his being dead in law have incapacitated him from reigning?

THE prince then had his ſentence read to him; and the ſame memoirs obſerve, that he fell into convulſions on hearing theſe words: "All laws divine and eccleſiaſtical, civil and military, condemn to death, without mercy, thoſe whoſe attempts againſt their father and their ſovereign have been fully proved." Theſe fits, it is ſaid, turned to an apoplexy, and it was with great difficulty he recovered.

ed. When he was brought to himself a little, and in the dreadful interval between life and death, he sent for his father to come to him: the Czar accordingly went, and both father and son burst into a flood of tears. The condemned prince asked his offended parent's pardon, which he gave him publicly; then being in the agonies of death, extreme unction was administered to him in the most solemn manner, and the day after the fatal sentence had been pronounced upon him, he died in the presence of the whole court. His body was immediately carried to the cathedral, where it lay in state, exposed to public view for four days; after which it was interred in the church belonging to the citadel, by the side of his late princess; the Czar and Czarina assisting at the funeral ceremony.

We are here indispensably obliged to imitate, in some measure, the conduct of the Czar, that is, to submit to the judgment of the public, the facts which we have related with the most scrupulous exactness, and not only the facts themselves, but likewise the various reports which were spread in relation to them, by authors of the best repute. Lamberti, the most impartial of any writer on this subject, and at the same time the most exact, and who has confined himself to the simple narrative of the original and authentic pieces relating to the affairs of Europe, seems in this matter to have departed from that impartiality and discernment for which

which he is so remarkable: for he thus expresses himself.

"The Czarina, ever fearful for the fortune of her own son, did not allow the Czar to rest, till she had obliged him to commence the proceedings against the Czarowitz, and to prosecute that unhappy prince to death; and what is still more extraordinary, the Czar, after having given him the kitout (which is a kind of torture) with his own hand, was himself his executioner, by cutting off his head, which was afterwards so fitted to the body, that it did not appear even to have been cut off, when it was exposed to public view. Some time afterwards, the Czarina's son died, to the inexpressible regret of her and the Czar. This latter, who had beheaded his own son, coming now to reflect, that he had no successor, contracted a sourness and morosity of temper. About the same time, he was informed, that the Czarina was engaged in a secret and criminal correspondence with prince Menzikoff. This, joined to the reflection, that she had been the cause of his putting to death his eldest son, made him conceive a design to strip her of the imperial honours, and shut her up in a convent, in the same manner as he had done his first wife, who is still living in that confinement. It was a custom with the Czar to keep a kind of diary of his private thoughts in his pocket-book, and he had accordingly entered therein a memorandum of this his design. The Czarina having found means to gain over to her interest all the pages of the Czar's bedchamber, one of them finding his pocket-book, which

he

he had carelessly left on the table, brought it to Catherine, who, upon reading this memorandum, communicated it to prince Menzikoff, and, in a day or two afterwards, the Czar was seized with an unknown violent distemper, of which he died. This distemper was atttributed to poison, on account of its being so sudden and violent, that it could not be supposed to proceed from a natural cause, and that the horrible act of poisoning was but too commonly used in Russia."

These accusations, thus handed down by Lamberti, were soon spread over Europe: and, as there still exist a greater number of pieces, both in print and manuscript, which may give a sanction to the belief of this fact to the latest posterity, I think it my duty to mention, in this place, what is come to my knowledge from unexceptionable authority.

I must therefore first declare, that the person who furnished Lamberti with this strange anecdote, was a native of Russia, but of foreign extraction, and who himself did not reside in that country at the time this event happened, having left it several years before. I formerly knew him; he had seen Lamberti, at the little town of Nyon, whither that writer had retired, and where I myself have often been. This very man owned to me, that he never told this story to Lamberti, but in the light of a report, which had been handed about at that time.

This instance may shew us, how much easier it was in former times, before the art of printing was found out, for one man to destroy the reputation of another, in the minds of whole nations, by reason that manuscript histories were in a few hands only, and not exposed to public reading, or to the observations of cotemporaries, as they now are. A single line in Tacitus or Suetonius, nay, even in the authors of the most fabulous legends, was enough to render a great prince odious to the half of mankind, and to perpetuate his name with infamy to posterity.

How could the Czar cut off the head of his son, when extreme unction was administred to him in the presence of the whole court? Had he no head when the sacred oil was poured upon it? When or how could this dissevered head be rejoined to its trunk? It is well known, that the prince was not left alone a single moment from the first reading of his sentence, to the time of his death.

BESIDES, this story of the Czar having had resource to the ax, acquits him at least of having made use of poison. It is somewhat uncommon, that a young man in the vigour of his days should die of a sudden fright, occasioned by hearing the sentence of his own death read to him, especially when it was a sentence that he expected; but after all, physicians will tell us that this is a thing that is possible.

IF the Czar had poisoned his son, as so many authors will persuade us, this would have deprived him of every advantage he might expect from this fatal process, in convincing all Europe that he had
a right

a right to punish every delinquent. It would have rendered all the reasons for pronouncing the condemnation of the Czarowitz suspected; and, in fact, accused himself. If he was resolved on the death of his son, he was in possession of full power to have caused the sentence to be put in execution: would a man of any prudence then, would a sovereign, on whom the eyes of all the world were fixed, have taken the base and dastardly method of poisoning the person whom he had a right to cut off with the sword of justice? Lastly, would he have suffered his name to have been transmitted to posterity as an assassin and a poisoner, when he could so easily have assumed the character of an upright, though severe, judge?

The result of all that I have revealed on this subject seems to be, that Peter was more the king than the parent; and that he sacrificed his own son to the sentiments of the father and law-giver of his country, and to the interest of his nation, who, without this unhappy rigour, were on the verge of relapsing again into that state from which he had taken them. It is plain that he did not sacrifice his son to the ambition of a step-mother, or the son he had by her, since he had often threatened to disinherit him, before Catherine brought him that other son, whose infirm state gave signs of a speedy death, which actually happened in a short time afterwards. Had Peter run such lengths merely to please his wife, he must have been a fool, or a weak timorous prince; neither of which, most certainly, could be laid to his charge. But he foresaw what would be the fate of his establishments, and consequently of his nation, if he had such a successor as would not prosecute his views. This prophecy is now verified: the Russian empire is become famous and respectable throughout Europe, from which it was before entirely separated; whereas, had the Czarowitz succeeded to the throne, every thing would have been destroyed. In fine, when this catastrophe comes to be maturely considered, the human heart shudders, and the severe approves.

This great and dreadful event is still fresh in the remembrance of the public; and it is frequently spoken of as a matter of so much astonishment, that it is absolutely necessary to examine what cotemporary writers have said of it. One of these hireling scribblers, who has taken on him the title of historian, speaks thus of it in a work which he has dedicated to count Bruhl, prime minister to his Polish majesty. "Russia was convinced that the Czarowitz owed his death to poison, which had been given him by his mother-in-law." But this accusation is overturned by the declaration which the Czar made to the duke of Holstein, that the empress Catherine had advised him to shut his son up in a monastery.

As to the poison which the empress is said to have given afterwards to her husband, that story is sufficiently destroyed by the simple relation of the affair of the page and pocket-book. What man would think of making such a memorandum as this, "I must remember to shut up my wife in a cona convent?" Is this a thing of so trivial a nature, that it must be set down lest it should be forgotten? If Catherine had poisoned her son-in-law and her husband, she would have committed crimes; whereas so far from being reproached for cruelty, she had a remarkable character for lenity and clemency.

It is now necessary to shew what was the first cause of the behaviour of Alexis, of his flight, and of his death, and that of his companions, who died by the hands of the executioner. It was owing then to mistaken notions in religion, and to a superstitious fondness for priests and monks. That this was the real source from whence all his misfortunes were derived, is sufficiently plain from his own confession, which we have already set before the reader, and in particular, by that expression of the emperor Peter in his letter to his son, "A corrupt priesthood will be able to turn you at pleasure."

The following is the manner in which a certain ambassador to the court of Russia explains these words. Many ecclesiastics, says he, tenacious of their ancient barbarous customs, and regretting the authority they had lost by the nation's having become more knowing and polished, wishing earnestly to see prince Alexis on the throne, from whose disposition they expected a return of those days of ignorance and superstition which were so dear to them. Among these was Dozitheus, bishop of Rostow. This prelate forged a revelation from St. Demetrius, and that the saint appeared to him, and had

had assured him as from God himself, that Peter would not live above three months; that the empress Eudocia, who was then confined in the convent of Sufdal (under the name of sister Helena) together with the princess Mary, the Czar's sister, should ascend the throne, and reign jointly with prince Alexis. Eudocia and Mary were weak enough to swallow this imposture, and were even so persuaded of the truth of the prediction, that the former quitted her habit and convent, and throwing aside the name of sister Helena, reassumed the imperial title and the ancient dress of the Czarina's, and caused the name of her rival Catherine to be expunged out of the liturgy. And when the lady abbess of the convent opposed these proceedings, Eudocia answered her haughtily, "that as Peter had punished the Strelitzes for affronting his mother, in like manner would prince Alexis punish those who had offered an indignity to his." She caused the abbess to be confined to her apartment. An officer named Stephen Glebo being introduced into the convent, she by presents brought this man over to her designs, and made use of him as an instrument to further her interest. He caused Dozitheus's prediction to be spread over the little town of Sufdal and the neighbourhood. But the three months being near expired, Eudocia reproached the bishop with the Czar's being still alive. "My father's sins, answered Dozitheus, have been the cause of this; he is still in purgatory, and has acquainted me therewith." Upon this Eudocia caused a thousand masses for him to be said, Dozitheus

zitheus assuring her that this would not fail of having the desired effect: but in about a month afterwards, he came to her and told, that his father's head was already out of purgatory. In a month afterwards he pretended he was freed as far as his waist, so that then he only stuck in purgatory by his feet; but as soon as they should be set free, which was the most difficult part of the business, the Czar would infallibly die.

The princess Mary, over persuaded by Dozitheus, gave herself up to him, on condition that his father should be immediately released from purgatory, and the prediction accomplished; and Glebo continued his usual correspondence with the former Czarina.

It was chiefly from a reliance on these predictions that the Czarowitz quitted the kingdom, and retired into a foreign country, to wait for the death of his father. However, the whole scheme soon transpired; Dozitheus and Glebo were taken into custody: the letters of the princess Mary to Dozitheus, and those of sister Helena to Glebo were publicly read in the open senate. In consequence of which the princess Mary was confined in the fortress of Schusselburg, and the old Czarina removed to another convent, where she was kept a close prisoner. Dozitheus and Glebo, together with the other accomplices in this fruitless and superstitious intrigue, were put to the torture, as were likewise the confidents of the Czarowitz's flight. His confessor, his preceptor, and the steward of the houshold, were all put to the torture, and died by the hands of the executioner.

Thus we see at what a dear rate Peter the Great purchased the happiness of his people, and such were the numberless obstacles he had to surmount in the midst of a long and difficult war without doors, and an unnatural rebellion at home. He observed one half of his family plotting against him, the majority of the priesthood obstinately bent to frustrate his schemes, and almost for a long time execrating its real happiness, of which as yet it was not become sensible. He had prejudices to overcome, and discontents to allay. In fine, there wanted a new generation formed by his care, who would at length entertain the proper ideas of prosperity and glory, which their fathers were not able to bear or comprehend.

CHAP. XI.

Works and Establishments in 1718, and the following years.

DURING the whole of the foregoing dreadful catastrophe, it plainly appears, that Peter had acted only as the father of his country, and that he considered the nation as his family. The punishments he had been obliged to inflict on such of them who had endeavoured to hinder the happiness of others, were necessary sacrifices, made for the general good.

IN this year*, which was the epoch of the disinheriting and death of his eldest son, was the time that he procured the greatest happiness to his subjects, by establishing a general police hitherto unknown, by the introduction or improvement of manufactures and works of every kind, by opening new branches of trade, which now began to flourish, by the making of canals, which joined rivers, seas, and people, when nature had separated them from each other. These indeed are none of the striking events which charm the bulk of readers: none of those court intrigues which are the food of malignity and malice, nor of those great revolutions which amuse the generality of mankind; but we see the real

* 1718.

springs of public happiness, which the philosophic eye delight to contemplate.

He now created a lieutenant-general of police over the whole empire, who was to reside at Petersburg, for maintaining good order from one end of the kingdom to the other. Luxury in dress, and the still more dangerous extravagance of gaming, were prohibited under severe penalties; schools for teaching arithmetic, which had been first set on foot in 1716, were now established in many towns in Russia The hospitals which had been begun were now finished, endowed, and filled with proper objects.

To these we may add the several useful establishments which had been projected some time before, and which were completed a few years afterwards. The great towns were now cleared of those innumerable swarms of beggars, who will not follow any other occupation but that of importuning those who are more industrious than themselves, and who lead a wretched and shameful life at the expence of others: an abuse too much overlooked in other nations.

The wealthy were obliged to build regular and handsome houses in Petersburg, agreeable to their circumstances, and, by a master-stroke of police, the several materials were brought carriage-free to the city, by the barks and waggons which returned empty from the neighbouring provinces.

Weights and measures were likewise fixed upon an uniform plan, in the same manner as the laws. This uniformity, so much, but in vain desired, fired, in states that have for many ages been polished, was settled in Russia without the least difficulty or murmuring; and yet I much question if this salutary regulation is practicable amongst us.

The prices of provisions were fixed. The city of Petersburg was well lighted with lamps, in imitation of those in Paris by Lewis XIV. and to which Rome is still a stranger. Engines were made for the speedy extinguishing of fire, the streets were well-paved, and rails put for the security of foot-passengers; in a word, every thing was provided that could minister safety, decency, and good order, and to the quicker dispatch and convenience of the inland trade of the country. Several privileges were granted to strangers, and proper laws enacted to prevent the abuse of those privileges. In consequence of these useful and salutary regulations, Petersburg and Moscow made a new appearance.

Manufactories for arms, iron, and steel works received additional improvements, particularly those which he himself had founded about ten miles distance from Petersburg, of which he himself was the first surveyor, and wherein no less than a thousand men were employed immediately under his inspection. He went in person to give directions to those who farmed the corn-mills, powder-mills, and mills for sawing timber, and to the managers of the manufactories for cordage and sail-cloth, to the brick-makers, slaters, and linen manufactories. Numbers of workmen in every branch came from France to settle under him;

him; this was one advantage of his journey to that kingdom.

He established a board of trade, the members of which were composed of one half natives, and the other half foreigners, in order that justice might be equally distributed to all artists and workmen. A Frenchman settled a manufactory for making fine looking-glass at Petersburg, with the assistance of prince Menzikoff. Another set up a loom for working fine tapestry, after the manner of the Gobelins; and this manufactory still meets with great encouragement. A third succeeded in the making of gold and silver thread, and to prevent the great consumption of bullion in the kingdom, the Czar ordered, that no more than four thousand merks of gold and silver should be expended in these works in the space of a year.

He gave thirty thousand rubles, that is, about one hundred and fifty thousand French livres, together with all the materials and instruments necessary for making the several kinds of woolen stuffs. By this useful bounty he was enabled to clothe all his troops with the cloth made in his own country; whereas, before that time, it was purchased from Berlin and other foreign kingdoms.

In Moscow they made as fine linen cloth as in Holland; and at his death Moscow and Jaronflaw had fourteen linen and canvas manufactures.

Who could imagine, at the time that silk sold in Europe for its weight in gold, that one day there would arise on the banks of the lake Ladoga, in the midst of a frozen region, and among unfrequented

quented marshes, a magnificent and opulent city, where the silks of Persia should be manufactured as well as at Ispahan. Peter understood and compleated this great work. The working of iron mines was carried to their highest degree of perfection; several other mines of gold and silver were discovered, and the council of mines was appointed to examine and determine, whether the working of these would bring in a profit equal to the expence of working them.

But to make so many different arts and manufactories flourish, and to establish so many various undertakings, it was not only alone sufficient to grant patents, or to appoint inspectors: it was necessary that our great founder should look into every thing himself, and in their infancy work at them with his own hands, in the same manner as we have already seen him working at the construction, the rigging, and the sailing of a ship. When canals were to be dug in marshy and almost impassable grounds, he was frequently seen at the head of the workmen, digging the earth, and carrying it away himself.

In this same year, 1718, he formed the plan of the canal and sluices of Ladoga: this was intended to make a communication between the Neva and another navigable river, in order for the more easy conveyance of merchandise to Petersburg, by avoiding the great circuit of the lake Ladoga, which, on account of the storms that prevailed on the coast, was frequently impassable for barks or small vessels. Peter levelled the ground himself, and they still preserve the tools which he used in digging

ging up and carrying off the earth. The whole court followed the example of the sovereign, and perfifted in a work, which, at the fame time, they looked upon as impracticable; and it was finifhed after his death; for not one of his projects, which had been found practicable, was abandoned.

The grand canal of Cronftadt, which is eafily drained of its waters, for careening and cleaning of men of war, was alfo begun at the time of his fon's trial.

In this year alfo he built the new city of Ladoga. Soon after he made the canal which unites the Cafpian Sea to the gulph of Finland and the ocean. The boats, after failing up the Wolga, came at firft to the waters of two rivers, which he made to communicate, and received from thence by another canal, they enter into the lake of Ilmen, and then fall into the canal of Ladoga, from whence goods and merchandizes may be exported by fea to all parts of the world.

In the midft of thefe labours, all carried on under his own eyes, his attention extended itfelf to a country in the moft eaftern parts of Afia, and caufed two forts to be built on thefe regions, fo long unknown to the reft of the world. In the mean time, a body of engineers, who were draughted from the marine academy eftablifhed in 1715, were employed all over the empire, in order to form exact charts thereof, and lay before mankind the vaft extent of country which he had civilized and enriched.

CHAP.

CHAP. XII.

Of the trade of Russia.

THE Russian trade was greatly decayed at Peter's accession to the throne; but he restored it anew. It is well known that the empire of trade has frequently shifted its seat in the world. The south part of Russia was, before the time of Tamerlane, the staple of Greece, and even of the Indies; and the principal factors were the Genoese. The Tanais and the Boristhenes were loaded with the productions of Asia; but when Tamerlane, towards the end of the fourteenth century, had conquered the Taurican Chersonese, afterwards called Crimea or Crim Tartary, and when the Turks became masters of Asoph, this great branch of trade was totally lost. Peter formed the design of reviving it, by getting possession of Asoph; but the unfortunate campaign of Pruth wrested this city out of his hands, and with it all his views on the Black Sea; nevertheless, he had it still in his power to open as extensive a road to commerce through the Caspian Sea. The English, who, in the end of the fifteenth, and the beginning of the sixteenth century, had opened a trade to Archangel, had endeavoured to do the same likewise by the Caspian Sea; but all their endeavours proved abortive.

It has been already observed, that Peter's father caused a ship to be built in Holland, to trade from Astracan to the coast of Persia This vessel was burnt by the rebel Stenkorazin, which destroyed all hopes of trading on a fair footing with the Persians The Armenians, who are the factors of that part of Asia, were admitted by Peter the Great into Astracan; every thing was obliged to pass through their hands, and they reaped all the advantage of that trade; as is the case with the Indian traders and the Banians, and with the Turks, as well as several nations in Christendom, and the Jews; for those, who have only one way of living, are generally very expert in that art on which they depend for a support; and others pay a voluntary tribute to that knowledge in which they know themselves deficient.

Peter had already found a remedy for this inconvenience, in the treaty which he made with the Sophi of Persia, by which all the silks, which was not used for the manufactories in that kingdom, were to be delivered to the Armenians of Astracan, who were to send it into Russia.

The troubles which arose in Persia soon overthrew this measure; and, in the sequel of this history, we shall see how the Sha, or emperor of Persia, Hussein, implored the assistance of Peter against his rebellious subjects; and how that monarch, after having supported a difficult war against the Turks and Swedes, entered Persia, and subjected three of its provinces. But to return to the article of trade.

Of

Of the Trade with CHINA.

THE scheme for establishing a trade with China seemed to promise the greatest advantages. Two vast countries bordering on each other, and each possessing what was wanting in the other, seemed to be both under the happy necessity of opening an useful correspondence, especially as a peace between Russia and China had been so solemnly ratified in the year 1689, according to our computation.

THE first foundation of this trade had been laid in the year 1689. There was at that time two companies of Siberian and Bukarian families settled in Siberia. Their caravans travelled through the Calmuck plains; after that they crossed the desarts to Chinese Tartary, and abundantly recompensed them for their great trouble and fatigue; but this trade came soon to an end by the troubles which happened in the country of the Calmucks, and the disputes between the Russians and Chinese, in regard to the frontiers.

AFTER the peace in 1689, it was natural for the two nations to fix on some neutral place, whither all the goods should be carried. The Siberians, like all other nations, stood in more need of the Chinese, than these latter did of them; accordingly permission was asked of the emperor of China, to send caravans to Pekin, which was readily granted in the beginning of the present century.

IT is worthy to be taken notice of, that the emperor Camhi had granted permission for a Russian church

church in the suburbs of Pekin; which church was to be served by Siberian priests, the whole at the emperor's own expence, who generously caused this church to be built for the accommodation of several families of eastern Siberia; some of whom had been prisoners before the peace of 1680; and the others were adventurers from their own country, who would not return back again after the peace of Niptchou. The agreeable climate of Pekin, the obliging manners of the Chinese, and the ease with which they found a handsome living, determined them to spend the rest of their days in China. This little Greek church could not become dangerous to the peace of the empire, as those of the Jesuits had been to that of other nations; and moreover, the emperor Camhi countenanced liberty of conscience. Toleration has, at all times, been the established custom in Asia, as it was in former times all over the world till the reign of the Roman emperor Theodosius I. The Russian families thus established in China, having intermarried with the natives, have since quitted the Christian religion, but their little church still remains

It was agreed, that this church should be for the use of those who come with the Siberian caravans, with furs and other commodities wanted at Pekin. The voyage out and home, and the stay in the country, generally took up three years. Prince Gagarin, governor of Siberia, was twenty years at the head of this trade. The caravans were sometimes very numerous; and it was difficult to

keep

keep the common people, who made the greatest number, in proper fubordination.

THEIR route lay through the territories of a Laman prieft, who is a kind of fovereign, refides on the fea-coaft of Orkon, and is ecclefiaftically ftiled Koutoukas; he is vicar of the grand Lama, but has rendered himfelf independent, by making fome change in the religion of the country, where the Indian tenet of metempfychofis is the prevailing opinion. We cannot find a more apt comparifon for this prieft, than in the bifhops of Lubeck and Ofnaburg, who have thrown off the Roman yoke. The caravans, in their march, fometimes committed depredations on the territories of this Tartarian prelate, as they did alfo on thofe of the Chinefe. This irregular conduct brought on a fecond interruption to the trade of thofe parts, for the Chinefe threatened to fhut the entrance into their empire againft the Ruffians, who brought from thence gold, filver, and precious ftones, in return for their merchandife. The largeft ruby in the world was brought out of China to prince Gagarin, who fent it to prince Menzikoff; and it now fhines in the imperial crown.

THE exactions of prince Gagarin were of great prejudice to that trade, which had brought him fo much riches; and, at length, they ended in his own deftruction; for he was accufed before the court of juftice, eftablifhed by the Czar, and fentenced to lofe his head a year after the condemnation of the Czarowitz, and the execution of all thofe who

who had been in connection with that unfortunate prince.

About the same time the emperor Camhi, perceiving his health decay, and knowing by experience, that the European mathematicians were much more learned in their art than those of his own nation, concluded, that the European physicians must also have more knowledge than those of Pekin, and therefore sent a message to the Czar, by some ambassadors who were returning from China to Petersburg, requesting him to send him one of his physicians. There happened at that time to be an English surgeon at Petersburg, who offered to undertake the journey in that character; and accordingly set out in company with a new ambassador, and one Laurence Lange, to whom we are obliged for a description of that journey. This embassy was received, and all the expences of it defrayed with great pomp by Camhi. The surgeon, at his arrival, found the emperor in perfect health, and gained the reputation of a most skilful physician. The caravans who followed this embassy made prodigious profits; but fresh excesses having been committed by this very caravan, the Chinese were so offended thereat, that they sent back Lange, who was at that time resident from the Czar at the Chinese court, and with him all the Russian merchants.

The emperor Camhi dying, he was succeeded by his son Yontchin, who had as great a share of wisdom, and more resolution than his father, and who drove the Jesuits out of his empire, as the Czar had

had done from Ruffia in 1718, concluded a treaty with Peter, by which the Ruffian caravans were to trade only on the frontiers of the two empires. None but the factors sent by the sovereign of Ruffia have liberty to enter Pekin, where they are lodged in a vast house, which the emperor of China formerly assigned to the envoys from Corea; but it is a considerable time since either caravans or factors have been sent from Ruffia thither; so that the trade, after being long in a declining way, is now upon the revival.

Of the trade of PETERSBURG, and the other ports of the RUSSIAN empire.

BY this time commerce was so greatly increased, that two hundred foreign vessels traded to the new capital, in the space of one year. This trade has continued increasing, and has frequently brought in five millions (French money) to the crown. This is much more than the interest of the money which this place had cost. This trade, however, greatly diminished that of Archangel, and was precisely what the founder intended; for the port of Archangel is too dangerous, and at too great a distance from other ports: besides that, a trade that is carried on immediately under the eye of an assiduous sovereign is always most advantageous. That of Livonia continued still on the same footing. The trade of Ruffia in general has proved very successful; its ports have received from one thousand to
one

one thousand two hundred vessels in a year, and Peter's abilities have annexed profit and glory together.

CHAP XIII.

Of the Laws.

IT is well known, that good laws are seldom to be met with, and that the due execution of them is still more so. It being very difficult to unite so large an empire, composed of such variety of people under the same body of laws, the father of the Czar Peter formed a digest or code under the title of *Oulogenia*, which was actually printed, but it by no means answered the end proposed.

PETER, in the course of his travels, had collected materials for rebuilding this great structure, which had fallen to decay in many parts. He gathered many useful materials from the government of Denmark, Sweden, England, Germany and France, selecting from each of these different nations what he thought would suit his own.

THERE was a court of boyars, who in processes judged definitively. Rank and birth were the only qualifications for a seat in this assembly, instead of knowledge; and therefore this court was dissolved.

HE

He then instituted an attorney-general, with four assessors, in each of the governments of the empire. These were to have an eye on the conduct of the judges, whose decrees were subject to an appeal to the senate which he established. Each of these judges was furnished with a copy of the *Oulogenia*, with additions and necessary alterations, until a complete body of laws could be digested.

These judges were to receive no fees, upon pain of death; for fees, however moderate, are always an abusive tax on the fortunes and the properties of those concerned in law-suits. The Czar took care that the expences of the court were moderate, and the decisions speedy. The judges and their clerks had salaries appointed them out of the public treasury, and were not suffered to purchase their offices.

It was in the year 1718, at the very time that he was engaged in the process against his son, that he made the chief part of these regulations. The greatest part of his laws he borrowed from those of the Swedes, and he made no difficulty to admit to places in his courts of judicature such Swedish prisoners who were well versed in the laws of their own country, and who having learned the Russian language, were willing to reside in the empire.

The governor of each province and his assessors had the cognizance of private causes within such government; from them there was an appeal to the senate; and if any one, after having been condemned by the senate, appealed to the Czar himself, and such appeal was found unjust, he was punished with death: but to mitigate the rigour of this law, the Czar created a master of requests, who received the petitions of those who had affairs depending in the senate, or in the inferior courts, concerning which the laws then in force were not sufficiently explained.

At length, in 1722, he finished his new code, prohibiting all the judges, under pain of death, to deviate from it, or to set up their own private opinions in place of the general statutes This dreadful ordonnance is always posted up in all the courts of judicature of the empire.

He gave a new form to every thing; the ceremonials of company are his work. He settled the different ranks of men, according to their posts and employments, from the admiral and the field-marshal to the ensign, without any regard to birth.

Having always in his own mind, and willing to imprint it on those of his subjects, that services are preferable to pedigree, and desirous to impress this truth on the minds of his people, a certain rank was fixed for the women; and she who took a place in a public assembly, that did not properly belong to her, paid a fine.

By a still more useful regulation, every private soldier, on being made an officer, instantly became a gentleman; and a nobleman, if his character had been impeached in a court of justice, forfeited his nobility.

After several of the laws and regulations had been settled, it happened that the increase of towns, wealth, and population in the empire, new undertakings,

takings, and the creation of new employs, necessarily introduced a multitude of new affairs and unforeseen cases, where were all consequences of that success which attended the Czar in the general improvement of his dominions.

The empress Elizabeth compleated the body of the laws which her father had begun, and they are a proof of the mildness of her government.

CHAP. XIV.

Of Religion.

AT this time also Peter was greatly concerned to reform the clergy. He abolished the patriarchate, and by this act of authority had alienated the minds of the clergy. He was determined that the imperial power should be free and absolute, and that of the church respected, but submissive. His design was, to establish a council of religion, which should always subsist, but dependent on the sovereign, and that it should give no laws to the church, but what should be approved of by the head of the state, of which the church was a part. He was assisted in this undertaking by the archbishop of Novogorod, called Theophanes Procop, or Procopowitz, i. e. son of Procop.

This prelate was both learned and wise; his travels through the different parts of Europe had afforded him opportunities of remarks on the several abuses which reign amongst them. The Czar, who had himself been a witness of the same, had this great advantage in forming all his regulations, that he was possessed of an unlimited power to chuse what was useful, and reject what was dangerous. He laboured, in concert with the archbishop, in the years 1718 and 1719, to effect his design. He established a perpetual synod, to be composed of twelve members, partly bishops, and partly archpriests, all to be chosen by the sovereign. This council was afterwards augmented to fourteen.

The motives of this revolution were explained by the Czar in a preliminary discourse. The chief and most remarkable of these was, " That, under the administration of a synod of priests, there was less danger of troubles and insurrections, than under the government of a single ecclesiastical chief; because the common people, who are always prone to superstition, might, by seeing one head of the church, and another of the state, be led to believe that they were in fact two different powers." And hereupon he cites as an example, the divisions which so long subsisted between the crown and the priesthood, and which stained so many kingdoms with blood.

Peter thought, and openly declared, that the notion of two powers in a state, founded on the allegory of two swords, mentioned in the apostles, was absurd and erroneous.

This tribunal was invested with the ecclesiastical power of regulating penances and examining

into

into the morals and capacity of thofe nominated by the court of bifhopricks, to pafs a final fentence in all cafes relating to religion, in which it was the cuftom formerly to appeal to the patriarch, and alfo to take cognizance of the revenues of monafteries, and the diftribution of alms.

This fynod was ftiled *moft facred*, the fame which the patriarchs were wont to affume; and in fact the Czar feemed to have reftored the patriarchal dignity, though divided among fourteen members, who were all dependent on the crown, and were to take an oath of obedience, which the patriarchs never did. The members of this holy fynod, when met in affembly, had the fame rank as the fenators; but they were, like the fenate, all dependent on the prince. But neither this new form of church adminiftration, nor the ecclefiaftical code, were in full vigour till four years after its inftitution, namely in 1722. Peter at firft intended, that the fynod fhould have the prefentation of thofe whom they thought moft worthy to fill the vacant bifhopricks. Thefe were to be nominated by the emperor and confecrated by the fynod. Peter frequently prefided in perfon at the affembly. One day that a vacant fee was to be filled, the fynod obferved to the emperor, that they had none but ignorant perfons to prefent to his majefty: " Well then," replied the Czar, " you have only to pitch upon the moft honeft man, he will be worth two learned ones."

It is to be obferved, that the Greek church has no fecular abbots. The *fmall band* is unknown there, otherwife otherwise than by the ridiculousness of its character; but by another abuse (as every thing in this world must be subject to abuse) the bishops and prelates are all chosen from among the monasticks. The primitive monks were only laymen, partly devotees, and partly fanatics. St. Basil gathered them together, and gave them a body of rules, and then they took vows, and were reckoned as the lower order of the church, which is the first step to be taken to arise at higher dignities. Hence Greece and Asia were filled with monks. Russia was over-run with them. They became rich, powerful, and though grossly ignorant, they were, at the accession of Peter to the throne, almost the only persons who knew how to write. Of this knowledge they made such an abuse, when struck and confounded with the new regulations which Peter introduced in all the departments of government, that he was obliged in 1703 to issue an edict, forbidding the use of pen and ink to the monks, without an express order from the archimandrite, or prior of the convent, who in that case was responsible for the behaviour of those to whom he granted this indulgence.

Peter designed to make this a standing law, and at first he intended, that no one should be admitted into the monastic order under fifty years of age; but that appeared too late an age, as the life of man being in general so limited, there was not time sufficient for such persons to acquire the necessary qualifications for being made bishops; and therefore, with the advice of his synod, he reduced

it

it to thirty years compleat, but never under; at the same time expresly prohibiting every military person, or an occupier of land, to enter into a convent, without an express commission from the emperor or synod, and to admit no married man upon any account whatever, even though divorced from his wife, unless that wife should, at the same time, embrace a religious life of her own pure will, and that neither of them had any children. No person in actual employ under the government, can take the habit, without an express order of state for that purpose. Every monk is obliged to work with his hands at some trade. The female religious are never to go out of the convent, and at the age of fifty are to receive the tonsure, as did the deaconesses of the primitive church; but if, previous to that ceremony, they have an inclination to marry, they are not only allowed, but even exhorted to it. An admirable regulation in a country where population is much more wanted than monasteries!

PETER was desirous that those unhappy females, whom God has destined to people a kingdom, and who, by a mistaken devotion, buried, in cloisters, that race of which they would otherwise become mothers, should at least be of some service to society, thus injured by them: and therefore ordered, that they should all be employed in some handyworks, suitable to their sex. The empress Catherine took upon herself the care of sending for several handicrafts over from Brabant and Holland, whom she distributed among these convents, and, in a short time, they produced several kinds of fine laces,

laces, which the empress and her ladies always wore as a part of their dress.

There cannot perhaps be any thing conceived more prudent than these institutions; but what merits the attention of all ages, is the regulation which Peter made himself, and which he addressed to the synod in 1724. The ancient ecclesiastical institution is there very learnedly explained, and the indolence of the monkish life admirably well exposed; and it not only recommends but enjoins an application to labour and industry; and that the principal occupation of those people should be to assist and relieve the poor. He likewise orders, that disabled soldiers should be distributed in the convents, and that a certain number of monks shall be set apart to take care of them, and that the most strong and healthy of them should cultivate the lands belonging to these convents. He orders the same regulations to be observed in the nunneries for women, and that the strongest of these shall take care of the gardens, and the rest to wait on sick or infirm women who shall be brought from the neighbouring country into the convent. He also enters into the minutest details relating to these services: and lastly, he appoints certain monasteries of both sexes for the reception and bringing up of orphans.

In the ordinance of Peter the Great, which was published the thirty first of January 1724, one would imagine it to have been framed by a minister of state and a father of the church.

Most of the customs in the Russian church are different

different from those of ours. As soon as a man is made a sub-deacon, he is prohibited to marry; and he is accounted guilty of sacrilege if he proves instrumental to the population of his country. On the contrary, when any one has taken a sub-deacon's orders in Russia, he is obliged likewise to take a wife, and thus he is capable of being a priest, and archpriest; but a bishop must be a widower and a monk.

Peter prohibited all priests from bringing up more than one son to the service of their church, unless it was at the desire of the parish; and this he did, lest a numerous family might in time come to tyrannize over the parish. We may perceive in these little circumstances relating to church government, that the legislator had always the good of the state in view, and that he took every precaution to make the priesthood properly respected, without being dangerous, and that they should neither be contemptible nor powerful.

In the very curious memoirs of an officer who was a particular favourite of Peter the Great, I find the following anecdote. One day a person reading to the Czar that number of the English Spectator, in which a parallel is drawn between him and Lewis XIV. "I do not think," said Peter, "that I deserve the preference that is here given me over that monarch; but I have been fortunate enough to have the superiority over him in one essential point, namely, of having brought my clergy to be submissive and quiet, and Lewis has suffered his to get the better of him."

To a prince, whose days were almost wholly spent in military labours, and his nights in the compiling laws for the better government of so vast an empire, and in directing so many immense works through a space of two thousand leagues, some relaxations were necessary. Diversions at that time were neither so noble nor elegant as they now are, and therefore we must not wonder if Peter amused himself with the entertainment of his farce of Cardinals, of which mention has been already made, and other diversions in that taste, which were frequently at the expence of the Romish church, to which he had a great aversion, and which was very pardonable in a prince of the Greek communion, who was determined to be master in his own dominions. He likewise gave several interludes of the same kind at the expence of the monks of his own country, but of the antient monks, whose follies and bigotry he wished to ridicule, while he strove to reform the new.

We have already seen how Peter the Great, previous to his publishing his church-laws, created one of his fools Pope, and celebrated the feast of the sham conclave. This fool, whose name was Iotof, was between eighty and ninety. The Czar took it into his head to make him marry an old widow of his own age, and to have their nuptials publickly solemnized; he caused the invitation to the marriage guests to be made by four persons who were remarkable for stammering. The bride was conducted to church by decrepit old men: four of the most bulky men that could be found in Russia acted

acted as running footmen. The music were seated in a waggon drawn by bears, whom they every now and then pricked with goads of iron, and who, by their roaring, formed a full bafe, perfectly agreeable to the concert in the cart. The married couple received the benediction in the cathedral from the hands of a deaf and blind prieft, who, to appear more ridiculous, wore a large pair of spectacles on his nose. The proceffion, the wedding, the marriage feaft, the undreffing of the bride, and the bride-groom, and putting them to bed, were all of a piece with the reft of this burleque ceremony.

We may perhaps be apt to look upon this as a very trivial and ridiculous entertainment for a great prince; but is it more fo than our carnival? or to fee five or fix hundred perfons with mafks on their faces, and dreffed in the moft ridiculous manner, fkipping and jumping about together for a whole night in a large room, without a fingle word of difcourfe?

In fine, were the ancient feafts of the Fools and the Afs, and the Abbot of the Cuckolds, which were formerly reprefented in our churches, much fuperior? or did our comedies of the Foolifh Mother exhibit marks of a greater genius?

CHAP. XV.

Negotiations in the isle of Aland. Death of Charles XII. The treaty of Nystadt.

THESE regulations of every particular concern, relating to so large an empire, and the melancholy trial and catastrophe of prince Alexis, were not the only concerns that employed Peter's enlarged mind; he not only established peace at home, but secured his empire from foreign danger. The war with Sweden was still carried on, though with less vigour, in hopes of a speedy peace.

It is a certain fact, that, in the year 1717, Cardinal Alberoni, prime minister to Philip V. of Spain, and baron Goertz, who had gained an entire ascendant over the mind of Charles XII had concerted a project to change the face of affairs in Europe, by effecting a reconciliation between Charles and the Czar, dethroning George I. and replacing Stanislaus on the throne of Poland, while Cardinal Alberoni was to procure the regency of France for his master Philip. Alberoni had entered into a negotiation with prince Kourakin, the Czar's ambassador at the Hague, by means of the Spanish ambassador Baretti Landi, a native of Mantua,

tua, whom fortune had, like the cardinal, transported into Spain.

THE design of these foreigners was to overturn the general system, for masters to whom they were not born subject, or rather for themselves. Charles XII. gave into all these projects, and the Czar contented himself with taking them into private consideration. Since the year 1716, he made only feint efforts against Sweden, and those rather with a view to compel that kingdom to purchase peace by the cession of the provinces he had conquered, than to crush it altogether.

THE baron Goertz, ever active in his projects, had prevailed on the Czar to send plenipotentiaries to the island of Aland, where the peace was to be negotiated. Bruce, a Scotchman, and grand master of the ordnance in Russia, and the famous Osterman, who was afterwards at the head of affairs, arrived at the place appointed for the congress exactly at the time that the Czarowitz was put under arrest at Moscow. Goertz and Gillemburg were already there on the part of Charles XII. both impatient to bring about a reconciliation between that prince and Peter, in order to be revenged on the king of England. It was a very strange circumstance that there should be a congress, and no cessation of arms. The Czar's fleet still continued hovering on the coast of Sweden, and taking the ships of that nation: the intention of which was to hasten a peace, which he knew the Swedes stood so much in need of, and which must prove highly glorious to Peter.

NOT-

NOTWITSTANDING the little hostilities which still continued, every thing had the marks of an approaching peace. The preliminaries began by mutual acts of generosity, which produce stronger effects than many hand-writings The Czar sent back marshal Erenschild, whom he had taken prisoner with his own hands, without ransom; and Charles in return did the same by Trubetskoy and Gollowin, who had continued prisoners in Sweden since the battle of Narva.

The negotiations went fast on, and a thorough change was to take place in the affairs of the north. Goertz proposed to Peter to put the duchy of Mecklenburg into his hands. Duke Charles its sovereign, who had married a daughter of Czar John, Peter's elder brother, was at variance with the nobility of the country, who had taken arms against him. And Peter, who had looked upon that prince as his brother-in-law, had an army in Mecklenburg ready to espouse his cause. The king of England, elector of Hanover, declared on the side of the nobles. Here was another opportunity of mortifying the king of England, by putting Peter in possession of Mecklenburg, who, being already master of Livonia, would by this means, in a short time, become more powerful in Germany than any of its electors. The duke of Mecklenburg was to have the duchy of Courland, and a part of Prussia at the expence of Poland, which was to have Staniflaus again for its king. Bremen and Verden were to return to Sweden: but it was only by force of arms that these provinces could be wrested out of the hands

of

of king George; accordingly Goertz's project was, as we have already said, to effect a firm union between Peter and Charles XII. and that not only by the peace, but by an offensive alliance, in which case they were to send an army into Scotland. Charles XII. after conquering Norway, was to make a descent on Great Britain, and he fondly imagined he should be able to set a new king on the throne of England, after having replaced another on that of Poland. Cardinal Alberoni promised both Peter and Charles to furnish them with subsidies. The fall of king George I. would, it was supposed, draw with it that of his ally the regent of France, who being thus left without support, was to fall a victim to the victorious arms of Spain, and the discontent of France.

ALBERONI and Goertz now thought themselves secure of throwing all Europe into confusion, when a cannon-ball, from the bastions of Frederickthall in Norway, confounded all their mighty projects. Charles XII. was killed, the Spanish fleet was beaten by that of England, the conspiracy which had been formed in France was discovered and quelled, Alberoni was driven out of Spain, and Goertz was beheaded at Stockholm; and of all this formidable league so lately made, the Czar alone retained his credit, who, by not having put himself in the power of any one, gave law to all his neighbours.

AFTER the death of Charles XII. there was an universal change of government in Sweden. Charles had governed with a despotic power, and his sister Urica was elected queen on express condition of

renouncing

renouncing arbitrary government. Charles intended to form an alliance with the Czar against England and its allies; and the new government of Sweden now joined with these allies against Peter.

The congress at Aland, however, was not dissolved; but the Swedes, now in league with the English, flattered themselves that the fleets of that nation sent into the Baltic would procure them a more advantageous peace. A body of Hanoverian troops entered the dominions of the duke of *Mecklenburg, but were soon driven from thence by Peter's forces

Peter likewise had a body of troops in Poland, which kept in awe both the party of Augustus, and that of Staniſlaus; and as to Sweden, he had a fleet always ready, either to make a defcent on their coasts, or oblige the Swedish government to hasten matters in the congreſs. This fleet consisted of twelve large ships of the line, and several lesser ones, besides frigates and galleys. The Czar served on board this fleet as vice-admiral, under the command of admiral Apraxin.

A squadron of this fleet signalized itself in the beginning against a Swedish squadron, and after an obstinate engagement took one ship of the line and two frigates. Peter, who constantly endeavoured, by every poſſible means, to encourage and improve a navy of his own formation gave sixty thousand French livres in money among the

* Feb. 1716.

officers

officers of this squadron, on this occasion, with several gold medals, besides conferring marks of honour on those who principally distinguished themselves.

AT this time also, an English fleet, under admiral Norris, came into the Baltic, for to protect the Swedes. Peter, who well knew how far he could depend on his new navy, was not to be intimidated by the English, but boldly kept the sea, and sent to know of the English admiral, if he was come only as a friend to the Swedes, or as an enemy to Russia. The admiral's answer was, that he had not any positive orders as yet from his court on that head; however, Peter, notwithstanding this equivocal answer, continued to keep the sea with his fleet.

THE English fleet, which was come only to shew itself, and thereby induce the Czar to grant more favourable conditions of peace to the Swedes, went to Copenhagen, and the Russians made some descents on the Swedish coast, and even in the neighbourhood of Stockholm, where they destroyed some copper mines, burnt fifteen thousand houses †, and did mischief enough to make the Swedes heartily wish for an immediate peace.

ACCORDINGLY the new queen of Sweden pressed the renewal of the negotiations. Osterman was sent to Stockholm, and matters continued in this uncertain situation during the whole year 1, 19.

THE ensuing year the prince of Hesse, husband to the queen of Sweden, and now become king by his consort's cession, began his reign by sending a

† July, 1719.

minister

minister to the court of Petersburg, in order to forward the so much desired peace; but the war was still going on in the midst of these negotiations.

The English fleet joined that of the Swedes, but without committing any hostilities, as there was no open rupture between the courts of Russia and England, and admiral Norris offered his master's mediation towards bringing about a peace; but as this offer was made sword-in-hand, it rather retarded than facilitated the negotiations. The coasts of Sweden, and those of the new Russian provinces in the Baltic, are so situated, that the former lay open to every insult, while an attack on the latter is very difficult. This was clearly seen when admiral Norris, after having thrown off the mask, made a descent in conjunction with the Swedish fleet on the little island in the province of Estonia ‡, called Narguen, which belonged to the Czar, where they only burnt a peasant's house; but the Russians at the same time made a descent near Wasa, and burnt forty one villages, and upwards of a thousand houses, and did an infinite deal of damage to the country round about. Prince Galitzin boarded and took our Swedish frigates: and the English admiral seemed to have come only to see how formidable the Czar had made his infant navy; for he had but just shewn himself in those seas, when the Swedish frigates were carried in triumph into the harbour of Cronslot, before Petersburg. On this occasion, methinks, the English did too much, if they came only as mediators, and too little, if enemies.

‡ June, 1720.

At length, the king of Sweden asked a suspension of arms *; and as he found the menaces of the English had stood him in no stead, he had recourse to the duke of Orleans, the French regent; and this prince, at once an ally of Russia and Sweden †, had the honour of bringing about a reconciliation between them. He sent Campredon his plenipotentiary to the court of Petersburg, and from thence to that of Stockholm. A congress was opened at Nystadt; but the Czar would not agree to a cessation of arms till matters were on the point of being concluded, and the plenipotentiaries ready to sign. He had an army in Finland ready to over-run the rest of that province, and his squadrons kept the coast in continual alarms, so that he was capable to dictate the peace: accordingly they subscribed to whatever he thought fit to demand. By this treaty he was to remain in perpetual possession of all that his arms had conquered, from the borders of Courland to the extremity of the gulph of Finland, and from thence again of the whole extent of the country of Kexholm, and that narrow slip of Finland which stretches out to the northward of the neighbourhood of Kexholm; so that he remained master of all Livonia, Estonia, Ingria, Carelia, with the country of Wyburg, and the neighbouring isles, which secured to him the sovereignty of the sea, as likewise of the isles of Oesel, Dago, Mona, and several others: the whole forming an extent of three thousand leagues of country, of unequal breadth, and

---

* November, 1720.   † February, 1721.

which

which altogether made a large kingdom, a sufficient reward for twenty years toils and fatigues.

The peace was signed by the Russian minister Osterman, and general Bruce, at Nystadt, the 10th of September, N S.

This event gave Peter great joy, as it freed him from keeping such large armies on the frontiers of Sweden, as also from any apprehensions on the part of England, or the neighbouring states, and left him at full liberty to bestow his whole attention to the new modelling of his empire, in which he had already so happily begun, and to cherish arts and commerce, which he had introduced among his subjects, at the expence of indefatigable labour and industry.

In the first transports of his joy, we find him writing in these terms to his plenipotentiaries: "You have drawn up the treaty as if we had done it ourselves, and sent it to you for the Swedes to sign. This glorious event shall be always kept up in our memory."

The triumphal festivals, with which the Czar had entertained his people, during the course of the war, were nothing to be compared to these rejoicings for the peace, which the whole empire received with unutterable satisfaction. The peace itself was the most glorious of all his triumphs; and what pleased more than all the pompous spectacles on the occasion, was a free pardon and general release granted to all prisoners, and a general remission of all sums due to the royal treasury for taxes throughout the whole empire, to the day of the publication

of

of the peace. In consequence of which a multitude of unhappy people, who had been confined in prison, were set at liberty; only those guilty of highway robbery, murder, or treason, were excepted out of the general pardon.

It was on this memorable occasion, that the senate decreed Peter the titles of *Great, Emperor, and Father of his country.* Count Golofkin, the high chancellor, made a speech to the Czar in the great cathedral, in the name of all the orders of the state, the senators crying aloud, three times, *Long live our emperor and father!* in which acclamations they were joined by the united voice of all the people. The ministers of France, Germany, Poland, Denmark, and the States-General, waited on him with their congratulations on the titles lately bestowed on him, and formally acknowledged for emperor him who had been always known in Holland by that title, ever since the battle of Pultowa. The names of *Father*, and of *Great.* which were certainly his due titles, were glorious; that of *Emperor* was only an honorary title, given by custom to the sovereigns of Germany, as titular kings of the Romans; and it requires time before such appellations come to be formally used by those courts where such forms are matters of mere ceremony. But Peter was in a short time after acknowledged emperor by all the states of Europe, excepting that of Poland, which was still distracted with troubles and factions; and the Pope, whose suffrage was become of very little consequence, since the court of Rome had

had lost its credit, and was looked upon as quite insignificant in the eyes of all the courts of Europe.

CHAP. XVI.

Conquests in Persia.

RUSSIA is so situated, as to oblige her to keep up some connections with all the nations lying about the fiftieth degree of north latitude. When under a weak government, she was made a prey of by Tartars, Swedes, and Poles; but when governed by a brave and resolute prince, she has always become formidable to all her neighbours. Peter began his reign by an advantageous treaty with China. He had made peace with the Swedes and the Turks, with whom he had been at war at the same time, and now designed to lead his victorious armies into Persia.

Persia had begun to fall into that deplorable state, in which we now behold her. Let us figure to ourselves the thirty years war in Germany, the times of the league, those of the massacre of St. Bartholomew, and the reigns of Charles VI. and king John in France, the civil wars in England, the long and horrible ravages of the whole Russian empire by the Tartars, or their invasion of China; and then we shall have some slight notion of the calamities under which the Persian empire has so long groaned.

By

By a weak and indolent prince on one side, and a powerful and enterprising subject on the other, a whole kingdom is soon plunged into such an abyss of disasters. Sha Huffein, sophi of Persia, a descendant of the great Sha Abbas, who was at this time on the throne, had given himself wholly up to luxury and voluptuousness: his prime minister committed innumerable acts of oppression and injustice, which this great prince winked at, and this was the foundation of forty years desolation and bloodshed.

Persia, like Turky, has several provinces, all governed in a different manner. She has subjects immediately under her dominion, vassals, tributary princes, and even nations, to whom the court was wont to pay a tribute, under the name of subsidies: for instance, the people of Daghestan, who inhabit the branches of mount Caucasus, to the westward of the Caspian Sea, which was formerly a part of the ancient Albania; for the names and limits of all those nations are changed. These are now called Lesgians, and are mountaineers, who are rather under the protection than under the dominion of Persia. To these the government paid subsidies, to defend the frontiers.

At the other extremity of the empire, towards India, was the prince of Candahar, who commanded a military body, called Afghans. This prince of Candahar was a vassal of Persia, as the hospodars of Walachia and Moldavia are of the Turkish empire. This vassalage was not hereditary, but an exact likeness of the antient feudal tenures established

blished throughout Europe, by the race of Tartars who overthrew the Roman empire The Afghan militia, under the prince of Candahar, was the fame with the Albanians on the coasts of the Caspian Sea, in the neighbourhood of Daghestan, and a mixture of Circaffians and Georgians, like the ancient Mamelucks, who made a conquest of Egypt. The name of Afghans is a corruption; Timur, whom we call Tamerlane, had led these people into India, and they remained settled in the province of Candahar, which sometimes belonged to the Mogul empire, and sometimes to that of Persia. It was these Afghans and Lesgians by whom this resolution was begun.

Mir-Weis, or Meriwi'z, intendant of the province, whose office was only to collect the tributes, affaffinated the prince of Candahar, raised the militia, and continued master of the province till his death, which happened in 1717. His brother came quietly to the succeffion, by paying a flight tribute to the Perfian court. But the fon of Mir-Weis, who inherited the ambition of his father, murdered his uncle, and attempted the conquest of the province This young man's name was Mir-Mahmoud, but he was known in Europe only by the name of his father, who had begun the rebellion. Mahmoud reinforced his Afghans by adding to them all the Guebres he could get together. These Guebres were a race of old Persians, who had formerly been disperfed by the caliph Omar, and who still continued attached to the religion of the Magi (so celebrated in the reign of Cyrus) and were

always

always secret enemies to the modern Persians. Having assembled his forces, Mahmoud marched into the heart of Persia, at the head of an hundred thousand soldiers.

At the same time the Lesgians or Albanians, who, on account of the troublesome times, had not received their subsidies from the court of Persia, came down from their mountains with an armed force, so that the flames of civil war were lighted up at both ends of the empire, and extended themselves even to the capital.

These Lesgians ravaged all that country which stretches along the western borders of the Caspian Sea, as far as Derbent, or the *Iron Gate*. In this country, now laid waste, is situated the city of Shamachi, about fifteen leagues distant from sea, and is said to have been the residence of Cyrus, and by the Greeks called Cyropolis, for we know nothing of the situation or names of these countries but what we have from the Greeks; but as the Persians never had a prince whom they called Cyrus, much less had they any town called Cyropolis. It is much in the same manner that the Jews, who commenced authors when they were settled in Alexandria, invented a city that they called Scythopolis, which they said was built by the Scythians in the neighbourhood of Judea, as if either Scythians or ancient Jews could have given Greek names to their towns.

Shamachi was a city of great wealth. The Armenians who inhabit in the neighbourhood of this part of the Persian empire, carried on an immense

mense traffic there, and Peter had lately established a company of Russian merchants at his own expence, which was afterwards greatly improved. The Lesgians made themselves masters of this city by surprize, plundered it, and put to death all the Russians who traded under the protection of Sha Hussein, after having stripped all their warehouses. The loss on this occasion was said to amount to four millions of rubles.

Peter sent immediately to demand satisfaction of the emperor Hussein, who was then disputing the throne with the rebel Mahmoud, who had then usurped it, and likewise of Mahmoud himself. The former of these was willing to do the Czar justice, the other refused it; Peter therefore resolved to do himself justice, and accordingly took advantage of the distractions of the empire.

Mir Mahmoud still pushed his conquests in Persia. The sophi hearing that the emperor of Russia was preparing to enter the Caspian Sea, in order to revenge the murder of his subjects at Shamachi, made private application to him, by the means of an Armenian, to take upon him at the same time to come and relieve Persia.

Peter had for a considerable time formed a project to make himself lord of the Caspian Sea, by means of a powerful naval force, and to turn the tide of commerce from Persia and a part of India through his own dominions. He had caused several parts of this sea to be sounded, the coasts to be surveyed, and exact charts made of the whole. He then set sail for the coast of Persia the 15th day

of

of May, 1722. Catherine accompanied him in this voyage, as she had done in the former. They sailed down the Wolga as far as the city of Astracan. From thence he hastened to give directions about carrying on the canals, which were to join the Caspian, the Baltic, and Euxine Seas, a work which has been partly accomplished under the reign of his grandson.

WHILE he was directing these works, the necessary provisions for his expedition were arrived in the Caspian Sea. He was to take with him twenty-two thousand foot, nine thousand dragoons, fifteen thousand Cossacks, and three thousand seamen, who were to work the ships, and act as mariners in making descents on the coast. The horse were to march over land through desarts where there was frequently no water to be had, and afterwards to pass over the mountains of Caucasus, where three hundred men were sufficient to stop the progress of a whole army; but Persia was then in such a distracted condition, that any thing might be attempted.

THE Czar sailed about an hundred leagues to the southward of Astracan, till he came to the little town of Andrehoff. It may appear extraordinary to hear of the name of Andrew on the coasts of the Hyrcanian Sea; but some Georgians, who were formerly a sect of Christians, were the founders of this town, which the Persians afterwards fortified; but it fell an easy prey to the Czar's arms. From thence he continued advancing by land into the province of Daghestan, and caused manifestos to be circulated in the Turkish and Persian languages. It was

was necessary to keep fair with the Ottoman Porte, who reckoned among its subjects, not only the Circassians and Georgians, who border upon this country, but also several powerful vassals, who had of late put themselves under the protection of the Porte.

AMONG those vassals, there was one very powerful, named Mahmoud d'Utmich, who stiled himself Sultan, and had the courage to attack the Czar's troops, by which he was totally defeated, and the story says, that his whole country was made a bonfire.

PETER arrived soon at the city of Derbent *, by the Persians and Turks called Demir Capi, that is, the Iron Gate, and so named from having formerly had an iron gate at the south entrance. It is a long narrow town, its upper part joins a rocky branch of mount Caucasus, and the walls of the lower part are washed by the sea, which in stormy weather makes a breach over them. These walls may justly pass for one of the wonders of antiquity, being forty feet in height, and six in breadth, defended with square towers at the distance of every fifty feet. The whole work seems one uniform piece, and is built of a sort of brown free-stone mixed with pounded shells, which served as mortar, so that the whole forms a mass harder than marble. The city lies open from the sea, but that part of it next the land appears impregnable. There are still some ruins of an old wall like that of China, which

* September 14, 1722.

must

must have been built in the earliest times of antiquity, and stretched from the borders of the Caspian to the Black Sea; and this was probably a rampart raised by the ancient kings of Persia against those swarms of barbarian tribes which dwelt between these two seas.

According to the Persian tradition, the city of Derbent was partly repaired and fortified by Alexander the Great. Arrian and Quintus Curtius say, that Alexander did actually rebuild this city. They indeed add, that it was on the banks of the Tanais, because in their time the Greeks gave the name of Tanais to the river Cyrus, which runs by the city. It would be a contradiction to suppose that Alexander should build an harbour in the Caspian Sea, on a river that opens into the Black Sea.

There were formerly three or four other ports in different parts of the Caspian Sea. All which were probably built for the same end: for the several nations inhabiting to the west, east, and north of that sea, have in all times been barbarians, who had rendered themselves formidable to the rest of the world, and from hence principally issued those swarms of conquerors who subdued Asia and Europe.

And here I must beg leave to observe, how much pleasure authors in all ages have taken to deceive mankind, and how much they have preferred a vain shew of eloquence to truth. Quintus Curtius puts into the mouths of Scythians an admirable speech, full of moderation, philosophy and magnanimity, as if the Tartars of these climates had been all so many sages, and that Alexander had not been the general nominated by the Greeks against the king of Persia, the lord of the greatest part of southern Scythia and the Indies. Other rhetoricians, thinking to imitate Quintus Curtius, have studied to make us look upon those savages of Caucasus and its dreary deserts, who lived wholly upon rapine and bloodshed, as the people in the world most remarkable for austere virtue and justice, and have painted Alexander, the avenger of Greece, and the conqueror of those who would have enslaved him and his country, as a public robber, who had laid waste the world without justice or reason.

Those writers do not consider, that these Tartars were never any other than destroyers, and that Alexander built towns in their own country; and in this respect I may presume to compare Peter the Great to Alexander; like him he was as active and indefatigable in his pursuits, a lover and a friend of the useful arts; he surpassed him as a law-giver, and like him endeavoured to change the tide of commerce in the world, and built and repaired as many towns as Alexander did.

On the approach of the Russian army, the governor of Derbent resolved to give up the place; whether he thought he was not able to defend it, or that he preferred the Czar's protection to that of the tyrant Mahmoud; but brought the silver keys of the town and citadel, and presented them to Peter, whose army peaceably entered the city, and then encamped on the sea-shore.

THE

The usurper Mahmoud, already master of great part of Persia, in vain endeavoured to prevent the Czar from taking possession of Derbent: he stirred up the neighbouring Tartars, and marched into Persia to the relief of the place, but too late, for Derbent was already in the hands of the Czar.

Peter however was not in a condition to push his successes any further at this time. The vessels which were bringing him a fresh supply of provisions, horses, and recruits, had been wrecked near Astracan, and the season too far spent. He therefore returned to Moscow †, which he entered in triumph; and after his arrival (according to the custom) gave a strict account of his expedition to the vice-Czar Romadanowski; thus keeping up this singular farce, which, says his eulogium, pronounced in the academy of sciences at Paris, ought to have been acted before all the monarchs of the earth.

Persia continued still to be divided between Hussein and the usurper Mahmoud. The first sought the protection of the Czar, and the other dreaded him as an avenger, who was come to wrest the fruits of his rebellion out of his hands. Mahmoud exerted all his endeavours to stir up the Ottoman Porte against Peter, and for this purpose sent an embassy to Constantinople, while the princes of Daghestan, who were under the protection of the grand signior, and who had been stript of their

† Janu. 5.

territories

territories by the victorious army of Peter, cried aloud for vengeance. The divan was now alarmed for the safety of Georgia, which the Turks reckoned a part of their dominions.

The grand fignior was on the point of declaring war against the Czar, but was prevented by the courts of Vienna and Paris. The emperor of Germany at the same time declared, that if Ruſſia ſhould be attacked by the Turks, he ſhould be obliged to join in the defence of it. The marquis de Bonac, the French ambaſſador at Conſtantinople, made a dexterous uſe of the menaces of the Imperial court, and at the same time inſinuated, that it was contrary to the true intereſts of the Turkiſh empire, to ſuffer a rebel and an uſurper to ſet the example of dethroning ſovereigns, and that the Czar had done no more than what the grand fignior himſelf ſhould have done.

During theſe critical negotiations, Mir· Mahmoud was advanced to the gates of Derbent, and had laid waſte all the neighbouring country, in order to diſtreſs the Ruſſian army. That part of ancient Hyrcania, now called Ghilan, was reduced to a deſert, and the inhabitants put themſelves under protection of the Ruſſians, whom they looked upon as their deliverers.

By this they followed the example of the ſophi himſelf. That unfortunate prince ſent a formal embaſſy to Peter the Great, to implore his aſſiſtance; but the ambaſſador was hardly departed, when the rebel Mir Mahmoud ſeized on Iſpahan and the perſon of his ſovereign.

Thamaseb,

Thamaseb, the son of the dethroned sophi, who was taken prisoner, found means to escape out of the tyrant's hands, and get together a body of troops, with which he gave the usurper battle. He seconded his father's entreaties to Peter the Great for his protection, and sent to the ambassador the same instructions which Sha Hussein had given him.

This ambassador, whose name was Ishmael Beg, found that his negotiations had proved successful, even before he arrived in person; for, on landing at Astracan, he learned that general Matuskin was set out with fresh troops to reinforce the army in Dagheftan. The city of Baku, which, with the Persians, gives to the Caspian Sea the name of the Sea of Baku, was not yet taken. The ambassador therefore gave the Russian general a letter for the inhabitants, in which he exhorted them in his master's name to submit to the emperor of Russia. The ambassador then proceeded for Petersburg, and general Matuskin departed to lay siege to the city of Baku. The Persian ambassador arrived at the Czar's court the very day that tidings were brought of the reduction of that city *.

Baku is situated near Shamachi, where the Russian factors had been massacred, but is neither so well peopled, nor so rich as the latter. It is chiefly remarkable for the naptha, with which it furnishes all Persia. Never was treaty so speedily concluded as that of Ishmael Beg †. Czar Peter

* Aug. 1722. † Sept. 1723.

promised

promised to march with his forces into Persia, in order to revenge the death of his subjects, and to succour Thamaseb against the usurper of his crown; and the new sophi in return was to cede to him not only the towns of Baku and Derbent, but likewise the provinces of Ghilan, Mazanderan, and Asterabath.

Ghilan is, as we have already noticed, the ancient South Hyrcania; Mazanderan, which joins to it, is the country of the Mardi; and Asterabath borders upon Mazanderan. These were the three principal provinces of the ancient Median kings; so that Peter beheld himself, by the means of arms and treaties, in possession of Cyrus's first kingdom.

It may not be useless to our subject to observe, that, by the articles of this convention, the prices of necessaries to be furnished to the army were settled. A camel was to cost only sixty franks (about twelve rubles;) a pound of bread no more than five farthings, the same weight of beef about six. These prices furnish a convincing proof of the plenty he found in these countries, that possessions in land are of the most intrinsic value, and that money, which is only of nominal worth, was at that time very scarce.

Such was the miserable state to which Persia was then reduced, that the unfortunate sophi Thamaseb, a wanderer in his own kingdom, and flying before the face of the rebel Mahmoud, who had dipt his hands in the blood of his father and his brothers, was reduced to supplicate both Russia and Turky

to

to accept of one part of his dominions to preserve the other for him.

It was agreed then, between the emperor Peter, sultan Achmet III and the sophi Thamaseb, that the first of these should keep the three provinces above mentioned, and that the Porte should have Casbin, Tauris and Erivan, besides what she had already taken from the usurper. Thus was this fine kingdom dismembered at once by the Russians, the Turks, and the Persians themselves.

The emperor Peter's dominions now extended from the further part of the Baltic Sea, beyond the southern limits of the Caspian. Persia still continued a prey to revolutions and ravages, and its natives, till then opulent and polite, were now sunk in poverty and barbarism, while the Russian people had arisen from indigence and ignorance to a state of riches and learning. One single man, by a resolute and enterprizing genius, had brought his country out of obscurity; and another, by his weakness and indolence, had brought the ruin of his.

Hitherto we know very little of the private calamities which for so long a time spread desolation over the face of the Persian empire. It is reported, that Shah Hussein was brought so low by his misfortunes as to place with his own hands the tiara, or crown of Persia, on the head of the usurper Mahmoud, and also that this Mahmoud afterwards went mad. Thus the lives of so many thousands of men depend on the caprice of a fool or a madman.

man. They add further, that Mahmoud, in one of his fits of madness, put to death with his own hand all the sons and nephews of Shah Huffein, to the number of an hundred; and that he caufed the gofpel of St. John to be read upon his head, in order to purify himfelf, and received a cure for his diforder. Thefe and fuch like Perfian fables have been publifhed by our monks, and afterwards printed in Paris.

The tyrant, after having murdered his uncle, was in his turn put to death by his nephew Efhreff, who was as cruel and bloody a tyrant as Mahmoud.

Sha Thamafeb ftill continued imploring the affiftance of Ruffia. This Thamafeb was affifted, and afterwards replaced on the throne by the famous Kouli Khan, and was again dethroned by his reftorer.

Those revolutions, together with the fubfequent wars between the Ruffians and Turks, in which Ruffia was victorious, the evacuating the three provinces in Perfia, which coft Ruffia more to keep them than they were worth, are events which do not concern Peter the Great, as they did not happen till feveral years after his death; it may be fufficient to obferve, that he finifhed his military courfe by adding three provinces to his empire on the fide next Perfia, after having juft before added the fame number on the frontiers of Sweden.

C H A P.

CHAP. XVII.

Of the Coronation of the Empress Catherine I. and the Death of Peter the Great.

PETER, at his return from his Persian expedition, found himself much abler than ever to be the arbiter of the North. He now openly declared himself the protector of the family of Charles XII. whose professed enemy he had been for eighteen years. He sent for the duke of Holstein, nephew to that monarch, to his court, promised him his eldest daughter in marriage, and began to make preparations for supporting him in his claims on the duchy of Holstein Sleswick, and even engaged himself so to do by a treaty of alliance, which he concluded with Sweden *.

He hastened to compleat the works he had begun all over his empire, to the further extremity of Kamtshatka; and for the better direction of them, erected an academy of sciences at Petersburg. The arts and manufactures flourished on every side, the navy was augmented, the army well paid and cloathed, and the laws properly observ'd and enforced. Peter was now in the zenith of his glory, and in profoun peace, which he was pleased to share with her, who, by retrieving the disas-

* February, 1724.

ter of the campaign of the Pruth, contributed to that glory.

The ceremony of the coronation of his confort Catherine was performed at Mofcow in prefence of the duchefs of Courland, his eldeft brother's daughter, and the duke of Holftein, his intended fon-in-law †. The manifefto which he publifhed on this occafion merits attention: he therein mentions the cuftoms of feveral Chriftian monarchs who had placed the crown on the heads of their conforts, producing inftances of the emperors Bafilides, Juftinius, Heraclius, and Leo the philofopher. He enumerates the important fervices Catherine had done to the ftate, and in particular in the war againft the Turks, where my army, fays he, which had been reduced to twenty-two thoufand men, had to encounter an enemy above two hundred thoufand ftrong. He does not fay in this declaration that the emprefs was to fucceed to the crown after his death; but this ceremony, which was altogether new and unufual in the Ruffian empire, was one of thofe means by which he prepared the minds of his fubjects for fuch an event. Another circumftance which might perhaps furnifh a ftronger reafon to believe that he defigned Catherine to fucceed him on the throne, was, that he himfelf marched on foot before her the day of her coronation, as captain of a new company which he had created, under the name of the *emprefs's knights*.

† May 28. 1724.

The ceremony was performed in the cathedral, and Peter himself placed the crown on her head; and when she would have fallen down and embraced his knees, he raised her; and at coming out of the church, caused the sceptre and globe to be carried before her. This ceremony was altogether worthy an emperor; for although in private life Peter loved plainness and simplicity, yet on public occasions he was magnificent and splendid.

Having thus crowned his spouse, he at length determined to give his eldest daughter Anna Petrowna in marriage to the duke of Holstein. This princess greatly resembled her father in the face, was very majestic, and of a singular beauty. She was betrothed to the duke of Holstein on the twenty fourth of November, 1724, but with very little ceremony. Peter had for some time past found his health declining, and this, together with some domestic uneasinesses, that perhaps heightened the distemper of which he died, took away all relish for feasts and public entertainments in the remaining part of his life.

The empress Catherine had at that time a handsome young man for the chamberlain of her household, whose name was Moens de la Croix, of a Flemish family †, but born in Russia, remarkably handsome and genteel. His sister, madame de Bale, was first dresser to the empress, and these two had entirely the government of her houshold. Being both accused of having taken presents, they were

† Memoirs of Bassewitz.

sent

sent to prison, and afterwards brought to their trial. The Czar, by an edict in the year 1714, had forbidden any one holding a place about court to receive any present or gratuity, on pain of infamy and death ; and this prohibition had been several times renewed.

The brother and the sister were found guilty, and all those who had either purchased their services or given them any gratuity in return for the same, were included therein, except the duke of Holstein and his minister count Bassewitz, as it is probable that the presents made by that prince to those who had brought about his marriage with the Czar's daughter were not looked upon in a criminal light

Moens was condemned to be beheaded, and his sister to receive eleven strokes of the knout. The two sons of this lady, one of whom was an officer in the houshold, and the other a page, were degraded, and sent to serve as private soldiers in the Persian army.

These severities, though they appear shocking to us, were perhaps necessary in a country where the observance of the laws is to be enforced only by the most terrifying rigour. The empress interceded for the lady's pardon ; but the Czar, offended at her application, peremptorily refused her, and in the heat of his passion, seeing a fine looking-glass in the apartment, he with one blow of his fist broke it into a thousand pieces ; and turning to the empress, "Thus," said he, "thou seest I can with one stroke of my hand reduce this glass to its

original

original duft." Catherine, in a foftening accent, replied, "It is true, you have deftroyed one of the greateft ornaments of your palace, but do you think it will become the finer for it?" This anfwer appeafed the emperor's wrath; but all the favour that Catherine could obtain for her dreffer was, that fhe fhould receive only five ftrokes of the knout inftead of eleven.

I SHOULD not have related this anecdote, had it not been related by a public minifter, who was eye-witnefs of the whole tranfaction, and who, by having made prefents to the unfortunate brother and fifter, was perhaps himfelf one of the principal caufes of their difgrace and fufferings. It was this affair which emboldened thofe who judge of every thing in the worft light, to fpread the report that Catherine fhortened the days of her hufband, whofe fits of paffion filled her with apprehenfions that overweighed the gratitude fhe owed for the many favours he had beftowed on her.

THESE cruel fufpicions were confirmed by Catherine's recalling to court her dreffer immediately upon the death of the Czar, and re-inftating her in her former favour It is the duty of an hiftorian to relate the public reports which have been circulated in all times in ftates, on the deceafe of princes who had been fnatched away by a premature death, as if nature was not alone fufficient to put a period to the exiftence of a crowned head; but it is the duty likewife of an hiftorian to fhew how far fuch reports were rafh or prefumptuous.

THERE

THERE is an immense difference between the momentary discontent which may arise from the passionate behaviour of a husband, and the desperate resolution of poisoning that husband, who is at the same time our sovereign and benefactor in the highest degree. The danger of such an attempt would have been as great as it was criminal. There was at that time a powerful party against her, who espoused the cause of the unfortunate Czarowitz. Yet, neither that faction, nor any one about the court, once suspected the Czarina; and the vague rumours which were spread on this head were founded only on the superficial notions of foreigners, who were very imperfectly acquainted with the affair, and who chose to indulge the wretched pleasure of accusing of heinous crimes those whom they thought were interested to commit them. But it was even very doubtful whether this was at all the case with Catherine. It was far from being certain that she was to succeed her husband. She had been crowned indeed, but only in the character of wife to the reigning sovereign, and not as one who was to enjoy the sovereignty after his decease.

PETER in his declaration had only ordered this coronation as a matter of ceremony, and not as conveying a right to the throne. He therein only quoted the examples of emperors, who had caused their consorts to be crowned, yet not one of them were ever invested with the sovereignty. Even at the very time of Peter's illness, several persons believed that the princess Anna Petrowna would succeed him

jointly

jointly with the duke of Holstein, her husband, or that the Czar would nominate his grandson for his successor; therefore, so far from Catherine's being interested in the death of the emperor, his preservation was of all things the most necessary for her.

It is undeniable, that Peter had, for a considerable time, been troubled with an abscess in the bladder, and a stoppage of urine. The mineral waters of Olnitz, and some others, which he had been advised to use, had proved of very little service to him, and he had found himself sensibly declining, ever since the beginning of the year 1724. His labours, from which he would not allow himself any respite, encreased his disorder, and hastened his end ‡: his malady become now more and more desperate; he felt burning pains, which threw him into an almost constant delirium. Whenever he had a moment's interval, he endeavoured to write, but he could only scrawl a few lines that were wholly unintelligible; and it was, with the greatest difficulty, that the following words, in the Russian language, could be distinguished, *Restore every thing to* †————

He then called for the princess Anna Petrowna, in order to dictate to her; but by that time she could come to his bed-side, he had lost his speech, and fell into a fit, which lasted sixteen hours. The empress Catherine did not leave him for three nights together. At length he expired in her arms, on

‡ Jan. 1725. † M. S. memoirs of the count de Bassewitz.

the

the twenty-eighth of January, about four o'clock in the morning.

The corpse was conveyed into the great hall of the palace, accompanied by all the imperial family, the senate, all the principal personages of state, and an innumerable concourse of people. It was there exposed on a bed of state, and every one was permitted to approach and kiss his hand, till the day of his interment, which was on the twenty-first of March 1725, N. S.

It has been thought, and it has been asserted in print, that he had named his consort Catherine to succeed him in the empire, by his last will: but the truth is, that he had made no will, or at least none that ever was seen; a most astonishing neglect in so great a legislator, and a proof that he did not think his disorder mortal.

No body knew, at the time of his death, who was to succeed him: he left behind him his grandson Peter, son of the unfortunate Alexis, and his eldest daughter Anna, married to the duke of Holstein. There was a considerable faction in favour of young Peter. But prince Menzikoff, who had never any other interests than those of the empress Catherine, took care to prevent any danger from either of the parties; and accordingly, when the Czar was just dying, he caused the empress to step into another apartment of the palace, where all their friends were assembled ready: he had the royal treasures conveyed into the citadel, and secured the guards in his interest, as likewise the archbishop of Novogorod, and then they held a private

private council, in presence of the empress Catherine, and one Maciroff a secretary, in whom they could confide, at which the duke of Holstein's minister assisted.

The empress left the council to return to her dying consort, who soon after yielded up the ghost in her arms. As soon as his death was made known, the principal senators and general officers repaired to the palace, where the empress made a speech to them, which prince Menzikoff answered in the name of the whole assembly. The empress being withdrawn, they proceeded to consider the proper forms to be observed on the occasion, when Theophanes, archbishop of Pleskow, told the assembly, that, on the eve of the coronation of the empress Catherine, the deceased Czar had declared to him, that his sole reason for placing the crown on her head was, that she might wear it after his death; upon which the assembly unanimously signed the proclamation, and Catherine succeeded her husband on the throne the very day of his demise.

Peter the Great was lamented in Russia by all those whom he had formed; and the generation of those who had been sticklers for the ancient customs soon began to look upon him as their father. Foreign nations, who have beheld the duration of his establishments, have always expressed the highest admiration for his memory, aknowledging that he was actuated by a more than common prudence and wisdom, and not by a vain desire of doing extraordinary things. All Europe allows that he
loved

loved glory, but that he placed it in doing good; that though he had faults, they never obscured his noble qualities; and that though, as a man, he was liable to errors, as a monarch he was always great: he every where forced nature, in his subjects, in himself, by sea and land; but he forced her only to render her more pleasing and noble. The arts, which he transplanted with his own hands into countries, till then in a manner savage, have flourished, and produced fruits which are lasting testimonies of his genius, and will render his memory immortal, since they now appear as natives of those places to which he introduced them. The laws, the police, politics, military discipline and navigation, commerce, manufactures, sciences, arts, all have been brought to perfection, answerable to his views, and by a singularity of which the whole world does not afford an instance: what he compleated has been kept up, what he begun has been compleated by four women who successively ascended the throne after him.

The court has undergone some revolutions since his death, but the empire has not suffered one. Its splendor was encreased by Catherine I. It triumphed over the Turks and the Swedes under Anna Petrowna; and under Elizabeth, it conquered Prussia and a part of Pomerania; and lastly, it has tasted the sweets of peace, and has seen the arts flourish in fulness and security in the reign of Catherine the second.

Let the historians of that nation enter into the minutest circumstances of the new creation, the

wars

wars and undertakings of Peter the Great: let them rouse the emulation of their countrymen, by celebrating those heroes who assisted this monarch in his labours, in the field, and in the cabinet. It is sufficient for a stranger, a disinterested admirer of merit, to have endeavoured to shew what that great man was, who left his kingdom twice to learn to govern them better, who learned from Charles XII. to conquer him, who, to set an example to his people, worked with his own hands, at almost all the useful and necessary arts, and who was the founder and father of his empire.

Sovereigns of states long since civilized, will say to themselves, "If a man in the frozen climates of ancient Scythia, assisted only by his own genius, has done such great things, what ought not we to do in kingdoms where the accumulated labours of many ages have rendered the way so easy?"

ORIGINAL

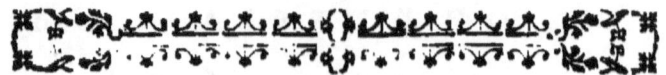

ORIGINAL PIECES,

According to the Translations made at their first publication, by order of Peter I.

CONDEMNATION of ALEXIS,
June twenty-fourth, 1718.

PURSUANT to the express command issued by his czarish majesty, and signed by his own hand on the thirteenth of June, for the trial of prince Alezis Petrowitz, in relation to his crimes and transgressions against his father and king; the undernamed senators, estates military and civil, after having assembled several times in the regency chamber of the senate of Petersburg, and having heard read the original writings and testimonies given against the Czarowitz, as also his majesty's admonitory letters to that prince, and his answers to them in his own writing, and other acts relative to the process, and likewise the criminal informations, declarations, and confessions of Alexis, partly written by himself, and partly delivered by word of mouth to his parent and king, before the several persons undernamed, appointed by his czarish majesty's majefty's authority to the effect of the prefent judgment, do acknowledge and declare, that though, according to the laws of the Ruffian empire, it belongs not to them, the natural fubjects of his czarifh majefty's fovereign dominions, to take cognizance of an affair of this kind, which for its importance depends on the abfolute will of the fovereign alone, whofe power, unlimited by any laws, is folely derived from God; yet in fubmiffion to his ordinance who hath given them this liberty, and after mature reflection, confcientioufly, without fear, flattery, or refpect of perfons, having nothing before our eyes but the divine laws applicable to the prefent cafe, both of the old and new teftament, the canons and rules of councils, the authority of the venerable fathers and doctors of the church, and taking alfo for their rule the inftructions of the archbifhops and clergy affembled at Peterfburg on this occafion, and conforming themfelves to the laws and conftitutions of this kingdom, which are agreeable to thofe of other nations, efpecially the Greeks and Romans, and other Chriftian princes; they unanimoufly agreed and pronounced that prince Alexis Petrowitz *deferves death*, for the aforefaid crimes and capital tranfgreffions againft his king and father, he being his czarifh majefty's fon and fubject; and notwithftanding the promife given by his czarifh majefty to the Czarowitz in a letter fent by M. Tolftoy and captain Romanzoff, dated from Spa, the twenty firft of July 1717, to forgive his elopement if he voluntarily returned, as the Czarowitz himfelf gratefully acknowledges in his answer to the letter dated from Naples the fourth of October 1717, wherein he thanks his majesty for the pardon he had promised him solely on condition of his speedy and voluntary return; yet he hath forfeited and rendered himself unworthy of that pardon, by renewing and continuing his former transgressions, as is set forth at large in his majesty's manifesto of the third of February in this present year, and because he did not return of his own accord.

And although his czarish majesty did, upon the Czarowitz's coming to Moscow, and his humbly confessing in writing his crimes, and begging pardon for them, take pity on him, as is natural for every father to act towards a son, and at the audience held in the great hall of the castle the same third day of February, did promise him full forgiveness for all his faults and transgressions, it was only upon condition that he would declare, without reserve or restriction, all his designs, and who were his counsellors and accomplices therein; but that if he concealed any one person or thing, that in such a case the promised pardon should be null and void; which condition the Czarowitz did at that time accept and receive with all outward marks of gratitude and obedience, solemnly swearing on the holy cross and the blessed evangelists in the cathedral church.

The next day his czarish majesty confirmed to the Czarowitz in writing the said promise in the following interrogatories, and which his majesty caused

caused to be delivered to him, having first written at the beginning what follows:

"As you yesterday received your pardon on condition that you would confess all the circumstances of your flight, and every thing relating thereto, but if you concealed any part thereof, you should answer for it with your life, and as you have already made some confessions, it is expected of you for our more full satisfaction, and your own safety, to commit the same to writing, in such order as shall in the course of your examination be pointed out to you."

AND at the conclusion, under the seventh article, there was again written with his czarish majesty's own hand.

"DECLARE to us every thing relating to this affair, though it be not mentioned, and clear yourself as if it were at confession; for if you conceal any thing that shall by any other means be afterwards discovered, do not impute the consequence to us, since you was yesterday told, that in such case the pardon you have received should be null and void."

NOTWITHSTANDING all which, the answers and confessions of prince Alexis were delivered without any sincerity; he not only concealed many of his accomplices, but also the capital circumstances relating to his own transgressions, particularly his rebellious designs in usurping the throne even in his father's life-time, flattering himself that the populace would declare in his favour: all this has since been discovered in the criminal process, cefs, after he had refufed to make a difcovery himfelf, as appeared above.

Thus it is evident by the whole conduct of Alexis, as well as by the confeffions which he both delivered in writing and by word of mouth particularly, that he was not difpofed to wait for the fucceffion in the manner which his father had left it to him after his death, according to equity, and the order of nature which God has eftablifhed; but intended to take the crown off the head of his father, while living, and fet it upon his own, not only by a domeftic rebellion, but by the affiftance of a foreign army, which he flattered himfelf to have at his difpofal, and to be purchafed even at the ruin of the ftate, and the alienation of every thing which might have been required of the ftate for fuch affiftance.

The above detail fhews, that the Czarowitz, in concealing all his pernicious defigns, and fecreting many perfons who acted in concert with him, as he continued to do till the laft examination, and till he was fully convicted of all his machinations, intended to referve to himfelf, on any opportunity, means of referving his defigns, and thoroughly to put in execution this horrid defign againft his father and fovereign, and againft all the kingdom.

The Czarowitz has already rendered himfelf unworthy of the pardon promifed him by his lord and father; he has alfo himfelf acknowledged, both before his Czarifh majefty and all the ftates, both ecclefiaftical and civil, and publicly before the whole affembly; and he has alfo, as well by word
of

of mouth as in writing, declared before the underwritten judges, appointed by his czarish majesty, that all the premises were true and manifest, by such effects as had already appeared; therefore, as the before-mentioned laws, divine and ecclesiastical, civil and military, condemn to death without mercy, not only those whose attempts against their father and king have been proved by testimonies and writings; but even such as have been convicted of an intention to rebel, and of having formed a design to murder their sovereign, and seize the empire; what shall we think of a rebellious design, almost unheard of in any history, joined to that of a horrid parricide, against him who was his father in a double capacity; a father of great kindness and indulgence, who brought up the Czarowitz from the cradle with more than paternal care and tenderness; who earnestly endeavoured to form him for government, and with incredible pains and unwearied application, to instruct him in the art of war, and qualify him to succeed to so large a kingdom? with how much stronger reason then does such an intention merit capital punishment?

It is therefore with afflicted hearts, and eyes full of tears, that we, as subjects and servants, pronounce this sentence; considering that it belongs not to us to give judgment in a case of so great importance, and especially to pronounce against our most bountiful sovereign lord the Czar's son. However, it being his pleasure, that we should act in this capacity, we, by these presents, declare

clare our real opinion, and pronounce the sentence of condemnation with a clear and Christian conscience, as we hope to be able to answer for it at the just, awful, and impartial tribunal of Almighty God.

We submit, however, this sentence, which we now pass, to the sovereign power, the will, and merciful revision of his czarish majesty, our most gracious king.

The PEACE of NYSTADT.

In the Name of the Most Holy and Undivided Trinity.

BE it known by these presents, that whereas a long, bloody and expensive war has arisen and subsisted for several years past, between his late majesty king Charles XII. of glorious memory, king of Sweden, of the Goths and Vandals, &c. his successor to the throne of Sweden, the lady Ulrica queen of Sweden, of the Goths and Vandals, &c and the kingdom of Sweden, on the one part; and between his czarish majesty Peter the first, emperor of all the Russias, &c. and the empire of Russia on the other part; the two powers have thought fit to exert their endeavours to find out means to put an end to those calamities, and prevent the further shedding of so much innocent blood;

blood; and it has pleased Divine Providence to dispose the minds of both powers, to appoint a meeting of their ministers plenipotentiary, to treat of, and conclude a firm, sincere and lasting peace, and eternal friendship between the two powers, their dominions, provinces, countries, vassals, subjects and inhabitants; namely, M. John Liliensted, one of the most honourable privy-council to his majesty the king of Sweden, his kingdom and chancery, and baron Otto Reinhold Stroemfeld, director of the copper-mines and fiefs of Daldars, on the part of his said majesty; and on the part of his czarish majesty, count Jacob Daniel Bruce, his aid-de-camp general, president of the college of mines and manufactories, and knight of the order of St. Andrew and the White Eagle, and M. Henry John Frederic Osterman, one of his said majesty's privy-counsellors in his chancery: which plenipotentiary ministers, being assembled at Nystadt, and having communicated to each other their respective commissions, and implored the divine assistance, did enter upon this important and salutary work, and have, by the grace and blessing of God, concluded the following peace between his czarish majesty and the crown of Sweden.

ART. I. THERE shall be from the present time, and for ever, a perpetual and inviolable peace, sincere union, and indissoluble friendship, between his majesty Frederic the first, king of Sweden, of the Goths and Vandals, his successors to the crown and kingdom of Sweden, his dominions, provinces,

countries,

countries, villages, vassals, subjects and inhabitants, as well within the Roman empire as out of the said empire, on one part; and his czarish majesty Peter the first, emperor of all the Russias, &c. his successors to the throne of Russia, and all his countries, villages, vassals, subjects, and inhabitants, on the other, in such wise, that, for the time to come, neither of the two reconciled powers shall commit, or suffer to be committed, any hostility, either privately or publicly, directly or indirectly, nor shall in any wise assist the enemies of each other, on any pretence whatever, or contract any alliance with them, that may be contrary to this peace, but shall always support and preserve a sincere friendship towards each other, and as much as in them lies, support their mutual honour, advantage and safety; as likewise prevent, to the utmost of their power, any disturbances or damages with which either of the reconciled parties may be threatned by any other power.

Art. II. It is moreover agreed upon betwixt both parties, that a general pardon and act of oblivion from all hostilities committed during the war, either by arms or otherwise, shall be strictly observed, so far as that neither party shall ever henceforth either remember, or take vengeance for the same, particularly in respect to persons of state, and subjects of any nation whatever, who have entered into the service of either of the two parties during the war, and have therefore become enemies to the other, excepting the Russian Cosaques, who enlisted in the service of the king of Sweden, and
whom

whom his czarish majesty will not consent to have included in the said general pardon, notwithstanding the intercession made for them by the king of Sweden.

ART. III. All hostilities, both by sea and land, shall cease both here and in the grand duchy of Finland in fifteen days, or sooner, if possible, after the signing of this peace; but in other places within three weeks, or sooner, if possible, after the necessary exchanges on both sides: and to this intent the conclusion of the peace shall be published without delay. And in case that, after the expiration of the said term, any hostilities should be committed by either party, either by sea or land, in any manner whatsoever, through ignorance of the conclusion of the peace, such offence shall by no means affect the conclusion of the said peace; on the contrary, both men and effects that may be taken after the said term are to be restored

ART. IV. His majesty the king of Sweden does, by the present treaty, both for himself and his successors to the throne and kingdom of Sweden, cede to his czarish majesty, and his successors to the Russian empire, in full, irrevocable and eternal possession, the provinces which have been taken by his czarish majesty's arms from the crown of Sweden during this war, viz. Livonia, Estonia, Ingria, and a part of Carelia; also the district of the fiefs of Wyburg, specified hereafter in the article for regulating the limits; the towns and fortresses of Riga, Dunamund, Pernau, Revel, Dorpt, Narva, Wyburg, Kexholm, and the other towns, fortresses, harbours,

harbours, countries, districts, rivers and coasts belonging to the provinces; as likewise the islands of Oesel, Dagoe, Moen, and all the other islands from the frontiers of Courland, towards the coasts of Livonia, Estonia, and Ingria, and on the east side of Revel, and in the road of Wyburg towards the south east, with all the present inhabitants of those islands, and of the aforesaid provinces, towns and countries; and in general, all their appurtenances, dependences, prerogatives, rights, and advantages, without any exception, as they were possessed by the crown of Sweden.

To which purpose, his majesty the king of Sweden renounces for ever in the most solemn manner, as well for his own part, as for his successors, and for the whole kingdom of Sweden, all pretensions which they ever had, or may have to the said provinces, islands, countries and towns; and all the inhabitants thereof shall, by virtue of these presents, be discharged from the oath of allegiance, which they have taken to the crown of Sweden, in such wise as that his Swedish majesty, and the kingdom of Sweden, shall never hereafter either claim or demand the same, on any pretence whatever; but, on the contrary, they shall be and continue incorporated for ever in the empire of Russia. Moreover, his Swedish majesty, and the kingdom of Sweden, promise by these presents to assist and support from henceforth his czarish majesty, and his successors to the empire of Russia, in the peaceable possession of the said provinces, islands, countries and towns, and that they will find out and deliver up to the

persons

persons authorized by his czarish majesty for that purpose, all the records and papers principally belonging to those places, which have been removed into Sweden during the war.

ART. V. His czarish majesty, in return, promises to evacuate and restore to his Swedish majesty, and the kingdom of Sweden, within the space of four weeks after the exchange of this treaty of peace, or sooner, if possible, the grand duchy of Finland, except only that part thereof which has been reserved by the following regulation of the limits which shall belong to his czarish majesty, so that his said czarish majesty, and his successors, never shall have or bring the least claim or demand on the said duchy, on any pretence whatever. His czarish majesty further declares and promises, that certain and prompt payment of two millions of crowns shall be made without any discount to the deputies of the king of Sweden, on condition that they produce and give sufficient receipts, as agreed upon; and the said payment shall be made in such coin as shall be agreed upon by a separate article, which shall be of equal force as if inserted here verbatim.

ART. VI His majesty the king of Sweden does further reserve to himself, with respect to trade, the liberty of buying corn yearly at Riga, Revel and Arensburg, to the amount of fifty thousand rubles; which corn shall be transported from thence into Sweden, without paying duty or any other taxes, on producing a certificate, shewing that such corn has been purchased for the use of his Swedish majesty, or by his subjects, charged with the care of making this purchase by his said majesty; and such right shall not be subject to, or depend on any exigency, wherein his czarish majesty may find it necessary, either on account of a bad harvest, or some other important reasons, to prohibit in general the exportation of grain to any place whatever.

ART. VII. His czarish majesty also promises, in the most solemn manner, that he will not interfere in the private affairs of the kingdom of Sweden, nor with the form of government, which has been regulated and established by the oath of allegiance, and unanimous consent of the states of the said kingdom; neither will he assist therein any person whatever, in any manner, directly or indirectly; but, on the contrary, will endeavour to hinder and prevent any disturbance happening, provided his czarish majesty has timely notice of the same, who will on all such occasions act as a sincere friend and good neighbour to the crown of Sweden.

ART. VIII. And the intention of both parties being to make a firm, sincere and lasting peace, to which purpose it is very necessary to regulate the limits so, that neither of the parties can harbour any jealousy, but that each shall peaceably possess whatever has been surrendered to him by this treaty of peace, they have thought proper to declare that the two empires shall from henceforth and for ever have the following limits, beginning on the northern coast of the Bothnic gulph, near Wickolax, from whence they shall extend to within half a league of the sea-coast inland, and from the distance

of half a league from the sea as far as opposite to
Willayoki, and from thence further inland; so that
from the sea-side, and opposite to Rohel, there shall
be a distance of about three quarters of a league, in
a direct line, to the road which leads from Wyburg, to Lapstrand, at three miles distance from
Wyburg, and which proceeds the same distance of
three leagues towards the north by Wyburg, in a
direct line to the former limits between Russia and
Sweden, even before the reduction of the district
of Kexholm under the government of the king of
Sweden. Those ancient limits extend eight leagues
towards the north, from thence they run in a strait
line through the district of Kexholm, to the place
where the harbour of Porogerai, which begins near
the town of Kudumagube, joins to the ancient limits between Russia and Sweden; so that his majesty the king, and kingdom of Sweden, shall
henceforth possess all that part lying west and north
beyond the above specified limits, and his czarish majesty and the empire of Russia all that part
which is situated east and south of the said limits.
And as his Czarish majesty surrenders from henceforth to his Swedish majesty and the kingdom of
Sweden, a part of the district of Kexholm, which
formerly belonged to the kingdom of Russia, he
most solemnly promises, in regard to himself and
successors to the throne of Russia, that he never
will make any future claim to this said district of
Kexholm, on any account whatever, but the said
district shall hereafter be and remain incorporated
into the kingdom of Sweden. As to the limits in

the

the country of Lampargue, they shall remain on the same footing as they were before the beginning of this war between the two empires. It is further agreed upon, that commissaries shall be appointed by each party, immediately after the ratification of this treaty, to settle the limits in the manner abovementioned.

ART. IX. His czarish majesty further promises to maintain all the inhabitants of the provinces of Livonia, Estonia, and Oesel, as well nobles as plebeians, and the towns, magistrates, companies, and trades, in the entire enjoyment of the same privileges, customs and prerogatives which they have enjoyed under the dominion of the king of Sweden.

ART. X. There shall not hereafter be any violence offered to the consciences of the inhabitants of the countries which have been ceded; on the contrary, his czarish majesty engages on his side to preserve and maintain the evangelical religion on the same footing as under the government of Sweden, provided likewise there is a free liberty of conscience allowed to those of the Greek religion.

ART. XI. As to the reductions and liquidations made in the reign of the late king of Sweden in Livonia, Estonia, and Oesel, to the great injury of the subjects and inhabitants of those countries, which, conformable to the justice of the affair in question, obliged his late majesty the king of Sweden, of glorious memory, to promise, by a proclamation, which was published the thirteenth day of April, 1700, " That if any one of his subjects could

could fairly prove, that the goods which had been confiscated were their property, justice should be done them;" and accordingly many subjects of the said countries have had such their confiscated effects restored to them; his czarish majesty engages and promises, that justice shall be done to every person, whether residing or not, who has a just claim or pretension to any lands in Livonia, Estonia, or the province of Oesel, and can make full proof thereof, and that such person shall be reinstated in the possession of his lands and effects.

Art. XII. There shall likewise be immediate restitution made, conformable to the general amnesty regulated and agreed in the second article, to such of the inhabitants of Livonia, Estonia, and the island of Oesel, who may during this war have joined the king of Sweden, together with all their effects, lands, and houses, which have been confiscated and given to others, as well in the towns of these provinces, as in those of Narva and Wyburg, notwithstanding they may have passed during the said war by inheritance or otherwise into other hands, without any exception or restraint, even though the proprietors should be actually in Sweden, either as prisoners or otherwise; and such restitution shall take place as soon as each person is re-naturalized by his respective government, and produces his documents relating to his right; on the other hand, these proprietors shall by no means lay claim to, or pretend to any part of the revenue, which may have been received by those who were in possession in consequence of the confiscation, on, nor to any other compensation for their losses in the war or otherwise. They who are thus restored to the possession of their effects and lands, shall be obliged to do homage to his czarish majesty, their present sovereign, and further to behave in every respect as faithful vassals and subjects; and when they have taken the usual oath of allegiance, they shall be at liberty to leave their own country to go and live in any other, which is in alliance and friendship with the Russian empire, as also to enter into the service of neutral powers, or to continue therein if already engaged, as they shall think fit. On the other hand, in regard to those, who do not chuse to do homage to his czarish majesty, they shall be allowed the space of three years from the publication of the peace, to sell or dispose of their goods, lands, and whatever belongs to them, to the best advantage, without paying any more than is paid by every other person, agreeably to the laws and statutes of the country. And if hereafter it shall happen that an inheritance shall devolve to any person according to the laws of the country, and that such person shall not as yet have taken the oath of fidelity to his czarish majesty, he shall in such case be obliged to take the same at the time of entering on the possession of his inheritance, otherwise to dispose of it in the space of one year.

LIKEWISE they who have advanced money on land in Livonia, Estonia, and the island of Oesel, and have lawful security for the same, shall enjoy their mortgages peaceably, until both capital and interests are discharged: on the other hand, the

mortgagees

mortgagees shall not claim any interests, which expired during the war, and which have not been demanded or paid; but those who in either of these cases have the administration of the said effects, shall be obliged to do homage to his Czarish majesty. This likewise extends to all those who remain in his czarish majesty's dominions, and who shall have the same liberty to dispose of their effects in Sweden, and in these countries which have been ceded to that crown by this peace. Moreover, the subjects of each of the reconciled powers shall be mutually supported in all their lawful claims and demands, whether on the public or individuals within the dominions of either of the two powers, and immediate justice shall be done them, so that every person may be reinstated in the possession of what justly belongs to him.

ART. XIII All contributions in money shall from the signing of this treaty cease in the grand dutchy of Finland, which his czarish majesty by the fifth article of this treaty cedes to his Swedish majesty and the kingdom of Sweden: on the other hand, the duchy of Finland shall furnish his czarish majesty's troops with the necessary provisions and forage *gratis*, until they shall have entirely evacuated the said duchy, on the same footing as has been hitherto practised; and his czarish majesty shall prohibit and forbid, under the severest penalties, the dislodging any ministers or peasants of the Finnish nation, contrary to their inclinations, or to do them any injury or damage. In consideration of which, and as it will be permitted his czarish majesty,

jesty, upon evacuating the said countries and towns, to take with him his great and small cannon, with their carriages and other appurtenances, and the magazines and other warlike stores which he shall think proper, the inhabitants shall furnish a sufficient number of horse and waggons, as far as the frontiers: and also if the whole of this cannot be executed according to the stipulated terms, and that any part of such artillery, &c. is necessitated to be left behind, then, and in such cases, that which is so left shall be properly taken care of, and afterwards delivered to his czarish majesty's deputies, whenever it shall be agreeable to them, and likewise be carried to the frontiers in manner as above. If his czarish majesty's troops shall have found and sent out of the country any deeds or papers belonging to the grand duchy of Finland, strict search shall be made for the same, and all of them that can be found shall be honestly given to his Swedish majesty's deputies.

ART. XIV. All the prisoners on both sides, of whatsoever nation, rank and condition, shall be set at liberty immediately after the ratification of this treaty, without any ransom; at the same time every prisoner shall either pay or give sufficient security for the payment of all debts by them contracted. The prisoners on each side shall be furnished with the necessary horses and waggons *gratis* during the time allotted for their return home, in proportion to the distance from the frontiers. In regard to such prisoners as shall have sided with one or the other party, or who shall chuse to settle in the kingdoms

doms of either of the two powers, they shall have full liberty so to do without restriction: and this liberty shall likewise extend to all those who have been compelled to serve either party during the war, who may in like manner remain where they are, or return home; except such who have voluntarily embraced the Greek religion in compliance to his czarish majesty; for which purpose each party shall cause the edicts to be published and made known in their respective dominions.

ART. XV. His majesty, and the republic of Poland, as allies to his Swedish majesty, are expresly included in this treaty of peace, and have equal right thereto, as if the treaty of peace between them and the crown of Sweden had been inserted here at full length; to which purpose all hostilities whatsoever shall cease in general throughout all the kingdoms, countries, and patrimonies belonging to the two reconciled parties, whether situated within or out of the Roman empire, and there shall be a firm and lasting peace established between the two said crowns. And as no plenipotentiary from his Polish majesty and the republic of Poland has assisted at this treaty of peace held at Nystadt, and that consequently they could not at the same time renew the peace by a solemn treaty between his majesty the king of Poland and the crown of Sweden; his majesty the king of Sweden does therefore engage and promise, that he will send plenipotentiaries to open the conferences, so soon as a place shall be appointed for the said meeting, in order to conclude, through the mediation

of

of his czarish majesty, a permanent peace between the two kingdoms, provided nothing is therein contained which may be prejudicial to this treaty of perpetual peace made with his czarish majesty.

ART. XVI. A free trade shall be regulated and established as soon as possible, which shall subsist both by sea and land between the two powers, their dominions, subjects and inhabitants, by means of a separate treaty on this head, to the good and advantage of their respective dominions; and in the mean time the subjects of Russia and Sweden shall have leave to trade freely in the empire of Russia and kingdom of Sweden, so soon as the treaty of peace is ratified, after paying the usual duties on the several kinds of merchandise; so that the subjects of Russia and Sweden shall reciprocally enjoy the same privileges and prerogatives as are enjoyed by the greatest friends of either of the said states.

ART. XVII. Restitution shall be made on both sides, after the ratification of the peace, not only of the magazines which were before the beginning of the war established in certain trading towns belonging to the two powers, but also liberty shall be reciprocally granted to the subjects of his czarish majesty and the king of Sweden, to establish warehouses in the towns, harbours, and other places under the dominion of his czarish majesty and the king of Sweden.

ART. XVIII. If any Swedish ships of war or merchant vessels shall have the misfortune to be wrecked, or stranded by bad weather, or any other accident, on the coasts and shores of Russia, his czarish

czarish majesty's subjects shall be obliged to give them all aid and assistance in their power to save the crews and effects, and faithfully to restore whatever may be cast on shore, if demanded, provided they are properly rewarded. And the subjects of his majesty the king of Sweden shall do the same in regard to such Russian ships and effects as may have the misfortune to be wrecked or otherwise lost on the coast of Sweden: for which purpose, and to prevent all ill treatment, stealing and plundering, which commonly happens on such calamitous accidents, his czarish majesty and the king of Sweden will issue a most rigorous prohibition, and all who shall be found transgressing in this point shall be exemplarily punished.

ART. XIX. And to prevent all possible cause or occasion of misunderstanding between the two parties, in relation to sea affairs, they have concluded and determined, that any Swedish ships of war, whether large or small, that shall hereafter pass by any of his czarish majesty's forts or castles, shall salute the same with their cannon, which compliment shall be directly returned in the same manner by the Russian fort or castle; and *vice versa*, any Russian ships of war, whether large or small, that shall hereafter pass by any fort or castle belonging to his Swedish majesty, shall salute the same with a discharge of their cannon, which compliment shall be instantly returned in the same manner by the Swedish fort; and in case any one or more Swedish and Russian ships shall meet at sea, or in any harbour, or elsewhere, they shall salute each

each other with a common difcharge, as is ufually practifed on fuch occafions between the Swedifh and Danifh fhips.

ART. XX. It is agreed on by both fides, no longer to defray the expences of the minifters of the two powers, as has been done hitherto; but their refpective minifters, plenipotentiaries, and envoys, fhall hereafter defray their own expences and thofe of their own attendants, as well on their journey as during their ftay, and back to their refpective place of refidence. On the other hand, either of the two parties, on receiving timely notice of the arrival of an envoy, fhall order that their fubjects give them all the affiftance they may ftand in need of to efcort them fafe on their journey.

ART. XXI. His majefty the king of Sweden does on his part comprehend the king of Great Britain in this treaty of peace, referving only the differences fubfifting between their czarifh and Britannic majefties, which they fhall immediately endeavour to terminate in a friendly manner; and fuch other powers, who fhall be named by the two reconciled parties within the fpace of three months, fhall likewife be included in this treaty of peace.

ART. XXII. In cafe any difference fhall hereafter happen between the ftates and fubjects of Sweden and Ruffia, it fhall by no means prejudice this treaty of perpetual peace; which fhall neverthelefs always be and remain in full force agreeable to its intent, and commiffaries fhall immediately be appointed on each fide to examine and adjuft all difputes.

ART.

ART. XXIII. All those who have been guilty of high treason, murder, theft, and other crimes, and those who deserted from Sweden to Russia, and from Russia to Sweden, either singly or with their wives and children, shall be immediately sent back, provided the complaining party of the country, from whence they made their escape, shall think fit to recall them, let them be of what nation soever, and in the same condition that they were at their arrival, together with their wives and children, as likewise with all they had stolen, plundered, or carried off with them when they went away.

ART. XXIV. The exchange of the ratifications of this treaty of peace shall be reciprocally made at Nystadt within the space of three weeks after the day of signing the same, or sooner if possible. In witness of all the premises, two copies of this treaty, exactly corresponding with each other, have been drawn up, and confirmed by the plenipotentiary ministers on both sides, pursuant to the authority they have received from their respective masters; which copies they have signed with their own hands, and sealed with their own seals. Given at Nystadt, the thirtieth day of August, in the year of our Lord 1721, O. S.

   JOHN LILIENSTED.
   OTTO-REINHOLD SROEMFELD.
   JACOB-DANIEL BRUCE.
   HENRY-JOHN-FREDERIC OSTERMAN.

Proclamation of the EMPEROR PETER I.

For the Coronation of the EMPRESS CATHERINE.

WE Peter I emperor and sole monarch of all Russia, &c. to all our officers, ecclesiastical, civil, and military, and all others of the Russian nation, our faithful subjects.

IT is universally known, that it has been a constant and invariable custom among the monarchs of all Christian states, to cause their consorts to be crowned, and that the same is at present practised, and hath frequently been in former ages by those emperors who professed the holy faith of the Greek church; to wit, by the emperor Basilides, who caused his consort Zenobia to be crowned; the emperor Justinian, his consort Lucipina; the emperor Heraclius, his consort Martina; the emperor Leo, the philosopher, his consort Maria; and several others, who have in like manner placed the imperial crown on the head of their consorts, and whom we shall make no mention of here, as it would carry us too far.

IT is also known how much we have exposed our own person, and faced the greatest dangers, for our country's cause, during the one and twenty years
course

course of the late war, which we have by the assistance of God terminated with such honour and advantage, that Russia hath never beheld such a peace, nor ever acquired so great glory as in the late war. Now the empress Catherine, our dearly beloved consort, having greatly comforted and assisted us during the war, and also in several other expeditions, wherein she voluntarily and carefully accompanied us, assisting us with her counsel and advice in every exigence, notwithstanding the weakness of her sex, particularly in the battle against the Turks on the banks of the river Pruth, wherein our army was reduced to twenty two thousand men, and that of the Turks amounted to two hundred and seventy thousand, and on which desperate occasion she signalized herself in a particular manner, by a courage and presence of mind superior to her sex, which is well known to all our army, and to the whole Russian empire: Therefore, for these reasons, and in virtue of the power which God has given us, we have resolved to honour our said consort with the imperial crown, as a reward for her good offices and fatigues; and we propose, by God's permission, that this ceremony shall be performed this winter at Moscow. And we do hereby give notice of this our resolution to all our faithful subjects, in favour of whom our imperial affection is unalterable.

THE END.

www.ingramcontent.com/pod-product-compliance
Lightning Source LLC
Chambersburg PA
CBHW031737230426
43669CB00007B/371